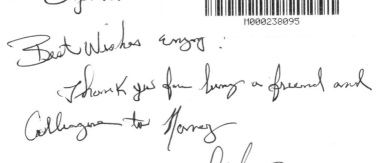

Investigating

the Death of Innocents

Investigating
the Death of Innocents

Det. Michael Orozco

IMAGO
P R E S S
TUCSON ARIZONA

Published in the United States of America by:

Imago Press
3710 East Edison
Tucson AZ 85716
www.imagobooks.com

Library of Congress Cataloging-in-Publication Data

Orozco, Michael.
  The death of innocents / Michael Orozco.
    p. cm.
  ISBN-13: 978-1-935437-22-2 (pbk. : alk. paper)
  ISBN-10: 1-935437-22-4 (pbk. : alk. paper)
  1. Murder--Arizona--Tucson--Case studies. 2. Child abuse--Arizona--Tucson--Case studies. 3. Children--Crimes against--Arizona--Tucson--Case studies. 4. Homicide investigation--Arizona--Tucson--Case studies. 5. Orozco, Michael. I. Title.
  HV6534.T8O76 2010
  364.152'3092--dc22
                         2010035193

Book and Cover Design by Leila Joiner

Cover photographs:
    Infinite corridor © alexfiodorov
    turned around © Simone van den Berg
    Little girl alone, afraid, hiding, feeling sad © Christophe Fouquin

ISBN 978-0-935437-22-2
ISBN 0-935437-22-4

Printed in the United States of America on Acid-Free Paper

This book is dedicated to all children. You are all good in this world, and you teach us in your innocent ways of what is right, honest, and what unconditional love is. Your love is the center that holds us true, and your voice is forever in heaven.

The promise of God to you is: "Let the children come to me and don't stop them, for the kingdom of God belongs to such as these." (Luke 18:16)

And to those who turn away the children: "Rescue those being taken off to death and save those stumbling towards slaughter. If you say, 'But we didn't know about this,' won't he who weighs hearts consider it? Won't he who protects life know? Won't he repay a person according to his works?" (Proverbs 24:11-12)

THE INVESTIGATORS

Front row, Left-right: Lt. Rick Hovden, Det. Michael Orozco, Analyst-Roxanne Stead, Det. Craig Arndt, Analyst-Kathy Martinjak, Det. Mike Walker.

Back row Left-right: Sgt. Carlos Valdez, Capt. Bill Richards, Det. Calvin Fuller, Crime Lab Technician Nora Rankin, Transcriptionist Deanna Mannino, Det. Sean Holewinski, not able to attend was Det. Lisa Lopez.

I've been a Tucson Police officer for twenty-five years, not including two years as a Tucson Police Department reserve officer. After my reserve time with TPD, I was hired by the South Tucson PD and worked with them for about two and a half years. In all, I spent ten and a half years as a patrol officer. In 1998 I was selected as a member of the TPD Hostage Negotiation Unit. I worked various assignments with TPD and was promoted to Detective on July 5, 2000.

After completing the detective training, I was assigned to the Dependent Child Unit (DCU) and have been with this unit ever since. I have, on occasion, been called to assist other units—the Adult Sexual Assault Unit, Homicide, Burglary, and others—in various capacities.

At TPD the average tenure for a child abuse detective is probably three to four years. I've been in the unit for ten years. It's what I do best, and I do feel that this was my calling in the department. There were times I almost left the unit to work another assignment but, for one reason or another, these never panned out. DCU is where I needed to be to best serve my community.

It's not the job for just anyone. I've seen detectives come into the unit and, after some exposure, they request to be transferred. This is okay, and I encourage the detectives to step forward if this is something they truly cannot handle.

I had one detective who had just come into the unit, and I was assigned to train him. I was working a homicide, and we were at the autopsy of a 20-month-old girl. As we were getting started on the autopsy, the detective backed up into a corner of the room. At the time, I didn't think too much about it. This little girl had severe closed-head trauma, and when the doctor exposed the subdural bleeds (a tearing, shearing, and bleeding of the bridging veins on the brain) and a skull fracture, I kept calling the new detective over to teach him what the injuries meant and what they looked like. I told him he needed to take notes and listen to the doctor's explanation of the injuries. The detective would come over, look, and then go back into the corner. He never did take notes or get the explanation or findings from the pathologist.

Afterwards, I spoke to him, and he told me he couldn't do this work. He said he had a child about the same age and knew this would affect him. He said he was worried about how the other detectives would feel if he left so soon. I said I understood and that this job was not for everyone. I told him not to worry about what the other detectives would think, because I would explain it to them. I told him the other detectives in our unit would be upset if we invested our time and effort to teach him, only to have him leave after he was trained. I told him it was better for him to separate now, rather than later. When we got back to the police station, I spoke to the sergeant and, within the week, the detective was moved to another unit. I told the detective I respected him for confiding in me and trusting me to do the right thing for him.

I must say it's been a pleasure to work with my colleagues in the Dependent Child Unit. I've been here the longest to date and have seen numerous detectives come and go. The people I've worked with are special in their own way, and this is partly because they deal with crimes against children. They're some of the finest and hardest working detectives within the police department itself. It's said that, if you can handle the work in this unit, then you can work any unit there is. It's the most demanding of any investigating unit.

The specialized training and knowledge that a detective needs to develop to work this assignment is unique. You have to develop a working medical knowledge to understand the complexities of the trauma that the children have suffered and to understand the doctor's explanations of that trauma. Once you understand the trauma, you then have to take that knowledge, see how it will apply to your investigation, and link everything together.

You will have an advantage while interrogating or interviewing the suspect because you can compare your understanding of the inflicted trauma to the suspect's given explanation. There are certain fractures (i.e., bucket fracture, corner fracture, spiral fracture, just to name a few) where the child is at a higher risk for having been physically abused. You remember to watch for these red flags.

In essence, you sort of become an integrated part of the medical field minus the medical degrees. Without this developed knowledge it would be harder to properly put together a complete investigation for prosecution. It's a slow learning process, and it takes a detective about two years to develop to the point of being truly effective. Again, these are the most complex of all investigations.

As a detective, I've either worked or been a part of numerous high profile child abuse investigations in the Tucson area. I've seen the impact these investigations have on the victim(s), the families, and the community. These investigations need to be the priority of any police department and community. They're the most important investigations and have a residual effect on any community. They affect everyone and touch our souls. The children are our future, and we need to protect them as much as possible. My personal opinion is that not enough emphasis is placed on investigations involving children, and the detectives working these crimes need to have proper training in order to be truly effective.

I've survived the stressors of these investigations and am often asked how I can do this type of job and handle it. I always reply that the job is not about me and never will be. It's about the children, who are our future and need to be protected against anyone who brings harm to them. When you look into the eyes of an injured child, they look to you for security, and trust that you will help them. We are the voice of the children whenever they are harmed or murdered. Too often, those in the community do not report suspected child abuse because they are not quite sure about what's going on or they don't wish to get involved. You need to get involved if you suspect something is wrong. Report it, and then let the authorities determine if it is child abuse. Protect the child!

It's not easy seeing the trauma that people inflict on children. Too many times I've looked into the eyes of dead children and babies, and each time it puts a stamp on your soul. My brother once said to me, "I bet you've become used to this by now." My reply to him was that you never get used to these types of investigations. At first, I was irritated by his remark, but I realized he doesn't understand what I do and how important it is.

Chuck Valenzuela is a psychologist and a friend of mine. He did advise me to seek counseling because of what I do. He said that, eventually, it would catch up to me in some way. He said the human mind and body isn't meant to deal with the horror and stress of these investigations. He said it's unnatural. He compared it to a soldier being in war and seeing the horror of the carnage around him. He said it would eventually take its toll on a person.

I believe him, because there are times when I see the investigations play out in my mind. I often relive them and think about the victimized children. I have shed tears for them, though I have never done this publicly. Every person who works these types of investigations understands this in some way. I believe that every person handles these investigations in their own personal way.

The first part of understanding these investigations is that children sometimes cannot verbally communicate with us to tell us how it is that they received their injuries or who caused them.

This could be due to their age, their medical condition, or because they have died. The injuries they have tell a story that leads to what happened or to the person or persons responsible for their injuries or death.

You must carefully examine the evidence in detail. You must carefully listen to the explanations given by the caretaker. If the person slips up and says something that doesn't coincide with the injuries, then something is not right with their explanation. It may be something minor, but you have to catch what they say and work it, either then or later. Timing is also very important, because you may want to hold onto that piece of information for later or confront them immediately. I've done it both ways.

Every child in the investigation is a crime scene, and you need to treat the child as such. This is where it gets difficult, because you have to examine every part of the child. Photographs and documentation of the injuries are very important, no matter where they are on the body. Photographs and documentation are just as important at an autopsy. The OME (Office of Medical Examiner) doctor should be able to give you an assessment of the injuries, including the manner and cause of death.

All detectives need to be patient and persistent while attempting to discover the cause of the trauma or death of the children or babies. If you pay attention to these details, then you will get the overall picture of the investigation and be able to work toward a successful conclusion. A successful investigation is not necessarily about prosecuting someone. It's about finding the truth and the cause of the injury or death, because sometimes it will be an accident. Keep an open mind.

If you find, during the course of an investigation, that the injury or death was accidental or due to a medical problem, then your investigation is as successful as prosecuting someone for non-accidental trauma. I always try to prove a person's explanation to be true; if I can't, then there will be a problem.

I know that people are very different, competitively speaking, and some are more competitive than others. I am driven to succeed and do not like to lose a case or leave one open. I'll do whatever I can—legally, of course—to put together a complete investigation for prosecution. I do not like working with detectives who don't put out this type of effort. I try to be as helpful as I can and teach newer detectives by sharing my experience. Most of the time, it's appreciated. I take a lot of heartfelt pride in these investigations.

My wife has told me that, whenever I work one of these investigations, I'm a different person. She has told me that, at times, I appear ambivalent toward her and at home. She tries to keep me balanced and keep me from thinking about the investigation while I'm at home and away from the office. I haven't told her enough times how much I do appreciate her keeping me in touch with her and the family. All I can say is that, whenever an investigation begins, I feel my responsibility to be the voice of these abused or murdered children. I switch into a different mindset.

As a successful detective, you have to keep an open mind to suggestions from your colleagues. If you're the lead detective in a case, you have a great responsibility to put the investigation together. Listen to the people around you; oftentimes, you might miss something because of the responsibility you carry, or you just might forget something.

The true story that I'm about to tell is about the patience and persistence with which we solved one of the most important child death investigations I've ever dealt with. This case will be with me for the rest of my life. This case has affected not only the victims and the families of the victims, but also the state of Arizona, the community of Tucson, and the Tucson Police Department.

This case was one of the mainstays of changing the state laws that protect our children. Arizona Child Protective Services will no longer be the same. Laws were changed to help account for the children in the system, so they will not be forgotten or slip through the cracks. Tyler and Ariana Payne were two children who fell through the cracks of the old system and were almost not accounted for at the time of their death. CPS failed to protect them against their father and his girlfriend.

This is a story that needs to be told for these precious children, to preserve their memory and to hopefully prevent such a tragedy from occurring again. This is the true investigation as it unveiled and progressed.

THE INVESTIGATION

ARIANA PAYNE

The Call & Scene

Day 1: Sunday, February 18, 2007

I'm home with my wife, Nancy, watching TV and doing small mundane chores around the house. Around 2:30 p.m. I receive a call from Det. Michael Walker. He asks me what I'm doing, and I tell him.

He says Sgt. Carlos Valdez called him to advise him that uniformed officers are out working the scene of a dead child. Valdez said he's going to call me. Carlos is fairly new with our unit. He's a very good supervisor, who listens to us and helps wherever he can.

Carlos told Mike that the remains of a child have been found in a container at a local storage unit at 519 E. Prince Road. I'm somewhat in disbelief and tell Mike I'm on my way. Carlos calls shortly after I get off the phone with Mike. He basically gives me the same information. Carlos says he's also going out on this one.

I tell my wife that, if this information is true, then this is going to be a lengthy investigation. I could be out for long time. She says she understands. I get dressed and kiss her as I leave to go to the storage facility. I then call Sgt. Valdez and tell him I'm on my way. He advises that he's also en route to the scene. He says he's received more information from the sergeant at the scene and has been told that the human remains were in a severe state of decomposition. The uniformed officers have secured the scene.

I arrive at about 1505 hours, and I'm the first detective to show up. I meet with Officer Ben Soltero, who is in training and is paired with Officer Bryan Bachtel. He tells me that, after he took the call, he responded and arrived at the storage facility. He met and spoke with Diane Hanselman, the daytime manager. She told him that, while she was cleaning out storage unit #C19, she removed a Rubbermaid plastic tub from the unit and dumped it inside the community Dumpster used by the storage facility. She told him that, as she removed the tub from the unit, she noticed a Tommy Hilfiger gym bag inside the tub and a foul odor emanating from either the gym bag or the Rubbermaid tub itself. This made her suspicious, so she decided to call 9-1-1. At the west end of the U-Store-It business, Diane pointed out the Tommy Hilfiger bag in the Rubbermaid tub that was inside the Dumpster.

Ofc. Soltero removed the tub that was inside Dumpster and placed it on the ground. He then took the Hilfiger bag out of the tub and placed it on the ground. He unzipped the bag and saw a black trash bag with one of the ends tied off in a knot. He knew something was inside the trash bag just by looking at it and by the weight of the bag. Ofc. Soltero then took a knife and cut an opening in the bag large enough to see inside. When he looked inside the bag, he saw the decomposing remains of a small child. He left everything where it was, backed off, and told Ofc. Bachtel what he had seen. The area was then secured with the yellow "Police Do Not Cross" tape. It was now officially a crime scene.

I see that Ofc. Soltero has done a good job up to this point, but I know I need to confirm his findings. I've been called to scenes in the past to confirm the possible remains of a child's body, only to discover an animal's remains instead.

I retrieve a pair of latex gloves and approach the Tommy Hilfiger bag to look inside the plastic bag. I spread open the section that has been cut and see what Ofc. Soltero has seen: the decomposing remains of a child. I note that the child is in a fetal position and, in my estimation, is that of a 3-year-old. I can't believe what I'm seeing. I am horrified and stunned, but I keep my emotions in check and walk out of the scene. I know there is serious work to be done.

By this time, Sgt. Valdez and Det. Mike Walker have arrived, so I tell them of my observation. TPD Commanders also arrive, and a briefing is conducted with everyone present. Capt. Bill Richards is new to CAPD (Crimes Against Persons Division). Capt. Richards was, at one time, a homicide detective who worked his way up through the ranks. He knows what has to be done and provides us with whatever resources we need. He mainly handles the media that will come and the commanders above him.

I'm assigned as the lead detective in this case because of the rotation schedule we use within our unit. Mike is my secondary detective. Our expertise is about to be tested as it's never been tested before. Just like most major investigations, where more than one commander shows up, they all want to voice their opinions and try to move you in the direction they feel the investigation needs to go. I see this happening, and I voice my opinion to Sgt. Valdez.

Carlos is put on the spot and advises me to just go with the flow for now; he will speak to Lt. Rick Hovden later. Lt. Hovden is the Lieutenant in our unit with Capt. Richards in our chain of command. I'm still irritated and have to calm myself down so I can focus on the investigation. Later, I find I appreciate the support we get from the command staff.

Assignments are then delegated, and it's decided that I will process the scene, conduct an interview with Ofc. Soltero, and then complete the initial police report. Mike is assigned to conduct an interview with Diane Hanselman and other potential witnesses. The TPD Crime Scene Specialists (CSS) are notified. Michael Herrera responds to photograph and assist in processing the scene. Dr. Erik Peters from the Office of the Medical Examiner is called and advised of the incident. He advises that he is responding to the scene.

The first thing I do is to conduct a recorded interview in my detective car with Ofc. Soltero. He states that at 1323 hours he received a suspicious activity call at 519 W. Prince Road (U-Store-It business) regarding a foul odor emanating from a plastic tub that had been removed from storage locker #Cl9. After his arrival, he spoke to the person who called in the report: the daytime manager, Diane Hanselman.

Ofc. Soltero says that Diane explained about the foul odor emanating from the tub and how she decided to throw it away. He says Diane told him that nothing spilled out when she put the tub inside the Dumpster. He says she took him over to the unit (#C19) and opened it. She showed him that nothing else was inside the unit. She then gave him the following timeline and events:

On 02-07-07 Ms. Hanselman went into the storage unit, cut the existing lock, and placed one of the company locks on the unit, so the items inside the unit would be available to be auctioned off. She placed the over-lock on the unit because of a failure to pay on the unit. She said when she opened the unit she saw that the Rubbermaid tub was the only item in the storage unit. She said there was a very strong foul odor coming from the tub. Afterwards, she closed the unit and locked it up.

On 02-16-07 Ms. Hanselman opened up unit #C19 again to get the item in the unit ready for the auction. While she was in the unit, she decided to sweep it out and complained to herself about the foul odor as she was cleaning it out. Afterwards, she locked it back up.

On 02/18/07 she went back into the storage unit to sweep it out again and get the item ready for the auction. She decided to throw it away because of the smell and removed the tub from the unit. After she placed the tub into the Dumpster, she decided to call the police.

I ask him if she told him what she did with the lock and the items that were swept away. Ofc. Soltero says he's not sure what she did with the lock or the contents she swept away. He says Ms. Hanselman has provided him with the file containing information about the last renter of unit #C19. He says he has the file, and later on he gives it to me. He goes into detail about how he removed the tub from inside the Dumpster and how he placed it in front of the Dumpster. He says that the tub was in an upright position when it was inside the Dumpster and that the lid was off. We don't go into much more detail.

After the interview is over, I briefly speak to Mike. He has interviewed Ms. Hanselman, and she told him that some of the liquid poured out of tub as she was dumping it and landed on her shoe and on the ground. Ofc. Soltero and I go over to the Dumpster area to process the scene after Mike gives me her information.

I first look at the tub and notice what appears to be some type of insect larvae inside it. I then make a visual observation inside the Dumpster and notice that it's about half full of debris. The lid to the Rubbermaid tub is lying on top of the debris, towards the back. I walk around the Dumpster and do not see any of the body fluid that supposedly was poured out by Diane.

I don't smell any odor from inside the Dumpster. However, I do notice that the odor is concentrated in the tub and the Tommy Hilfiger bag that is now on the ground. I continue to look inside the Dumpster for any dark liquid that might have settled, but don't see any of it.

I think about taking all of the items out of the Dumpster, but decide not to. It seems to me that all of the evidence presented—the tub, the lid, and the contents of the tub—had been sitting on top of the debris in the Dumpster. I have no other information causing me to think otherwise. Ms. Hanselman has stated that there was nothing else in storage unit #C19 when she went inside it on February 7, 16, and 18, 2007.

She has also said that she didn't hear anything roll out of the tub when she put the tub inside the Dumpster. My first thought is that I need to get to the body of the child. I don't see anything else out of the ordinary and do not pull out any of the garbage that has piled up in the Dumpster over the weekend. The inside and outside of the Dumpster are photographed by TPD CSS Mike Herrera.

I go back to the Rubbermaid tub and begin to process it for evidence. As I make my observation of the tub, I notice some type of cocoon besides the suspected insect larvae inside of it. CSS Herrera photographs these, and I take samples from the insides of the tub and lid.

I also notice several flow patterns inside the tub from when Ms. Hanselman was handling it and lifting it into the Dumpster with the body fluid sloshing around. At this time, the tub is not processed for any latent prints, but possibly will be at a later time. The items are later placed into property as evidence.

I then make a visual observation of the Tommy Hilfiger bag. I see what appears to be lines of the same type of insect larvae along the top of the canvas and zipper. These are photographed, and I collect samples of these larvae.

Dr. Eric Peters from OME arrives at the scene. He's given a briefing of the investigation and afterwards decides to examine the contents of the Tommy Hilfiger bag. The plastic garbage bag with the child's body is removed from the Hilfiger bag. As I lift the plastic bag, body fluid drips from the bottom of the bag into the Hilfiger bag. The plastic bag is then placed onto a large white sheet of paper.

Dr. Peters opens up the garbage bag, and the small body is rolled onto the paper. The body is in a fetal position and in a severe state of decomposition. It appears to be mummified, just skin and bones. The skin appears to be mushy, soft, and fragile, almost falling off the bones. It definitely has a foul odor.

Dr. Peters carefully stretches the legs out and takes a measurement; the body length is about 32 inches. He then looks at the hair and says it's a reddish-brown color. He estimates that the remains are of a 2- to 4-year-old white female child. Her mouth is open, and she looks to me as if she died in horror.

I think to myself that I cannot imagine the pain and suffering she went through. I know that, at this time, we don't know the cause of her death, but I feel inside that she must have suffered. Why else would someone try to hide her? I know this is bad and that she suffered.

I ask Dr. Peters if he can tell how long the child has been in the plastic bag. He says it's hard to tell because the plastic bag retains moisture, which affects the stages of decomposition. He says this child could have been inside the bag for a period of up to two years. He says he's going to consult with Dr. Bruce Anderson, the OME anthropologist, and get him involved.

I ask him about the suspected insects found in the bag. He says he's not an expert, but they do appear to be insects. He says that Dr. Bruce Anderson can probably make a better assessment of the insects. CSS Herrera takes photographs of the scene and the body. Dr. Peters takes custody of the child's remains, and an autopsy is scheduled for the following day.

I continue processing the scene and the following items collected from the Dumpster site are recorded as evidence. Evidence is identified by the initials of the person who collects it and places it into the property of evidence. Usually, you have a finder/collector and a recorder.

> #1-MPO-1-plastic container of suspected insect larvae
>   Rubbermaid lid
> #2-MPO-1-plastic container of suspected insect larvae
>   Rubbermaid tub
> #3-MPO-1-plastic container of suspected insect larvae
>   from TH bag
> #4-MPO-1-Blue plastic Rubbermaid Lid
> #5-MPO-1-Blue plastic Rubbermaid Tub
> #6-MPO-1-Tommy Hilfiger canvas athletic bag
> #7-MPO-1-Black plastic garbage bag

#8-MPO-1-plastic container of suspected cocoons from
   Rubbermaid tub
#25-MPO-1-purple file folder of storage unit C19 infor-
   mation – this file was kept out for research and later
   placed into property as the listed item number.

After the body and the Dumpster have been processed, I ask
Diane Hanselman to take me over to the storage maintenance unit
where the trashcan is located that she used to dispose of debris she
swept up and collected from unit #C19. She points out the tenant's
masterlock that was cut and removed from the unit. The following
items are collected from the trashcan:

#9-MPO-Plastic dust pan
#10-MPO-Broom/brush head
#11-MPO-Padlock

Another briefing is conducted with the command staff and
investigative team. Det. Walker advises that he has conducted
an audio-recorded interview with Diane Hanselman and Tracy
Letendre. Tracy is Diane's relief manager and works on the weekends. He relays the following information.

He tells us that unit #C19 was rented last September 2006, and
that the payments went into arrears. The management then sent
out default notices to the listed address. When there was no response to the default notices, the items in the storage unit were
going to be auctioned off.

He says that on 02/07/07 Diane and the auctioneers, Edward
and Casey Jones (mother and son), cut the lock that had been
placed on the unit by the renter and replaced it with one of the
company locks. At that time, they looked inside and noticed numerous bugs crawling on the floor and around the tub. They also
noticed that nothing else was in the storage unit and that a foul
odor was coming from the tub.

He says that Lori, another manager, went over and opened up the tub. She saw dark liquid at the bottom of it and a Tommy Hilfiger bag inside. She then closed it back up because of the foul odor coming from the tub. Ms. Jones then took an interior photograph of the unit, and the "over-lock" was then placed on the unit.

Ofc. Soltero has already given me the folder containing information regarding storage unit #C19. We review it and see the name, "Joshua Neuser," listed as the leaseholder of the rented locker. Mr. Neuser apparently rented the unit on 09/03/07 and had a listed address of 1729 E. Edison. Christopher Navarro, an ex-employee of U-Store-It, leased the unit to "Joshua Neuser."

After the briefing, Mike takes Dr. Peters over to storage unit #C19 for an observation. They don't collect any evidence because they don't see anything of evidentiary value. When I visit the storage unit later, I do see evidence and collect some items.

I stay at the scene and process the #C19 storage unit for more possible evidence. I scan the floor with my flashlight, looking for possible shoe prints and do see some shoe patterns. If you place the light parallel to the ground, patterns will light up. TPD CSS Michael Herrera takes photographs of the unit.

We notice that, at the southeast corner of the unit, there is what appears to be a rectangular, stained outline from body fluid that has seeped through the plastic of the tub. This is an indication of where the tub was placed inside the unit. I also see some pattern marks of unidentified stains around the tub stains. I notice a small rope used as a pull cord for the light fixture. All of these observations are photographed, and the following items are taken from the storage unit for evidence:

#MSH1-1-set of possible body fluid swabs taken from the floor the tub stains
#MSH2-1-set of possible body fluid swabs taken from the floor the tub stains

#MSH3-1-small rope light cord
#MSH4-1-set of latent prints from the exterior door
Photographs are taken of shoe patterns, shoes, and soles
    of Diane Hanselman
Photographs are taken of the storage unit and outline of
    the tub location

Carlos decides that more detectives are going to be needed to assist in the investigation. Detectives Lisa Lopez, Craig Arndt, and Sean Holewinski are notified and respond to the main police station. Carlos and Mike are also responding to the main station from the scene. I give Mike the U-Store-It file to conduct research on finding "Joshua Neuser" and to conduct an interview with him.

The Identifications

Still Day 1: Sunday, February 18, 2007

After the scene is processed, I respond to the main police station and meet with Carlos and the other detectives. They've done some research in reference to "Joshua Neuser," the applicant and lessee on storage unit #C19. Numerous possible locations are noted and assignments given in an attempt to find him and bring him in for questioning.

Officer James Stobbs works the uniformed division and is the beat officer for the area that we're looking in. He's called in from patrol to assist in the investigation. After he's briefed, he says he knows of a possible location where Joshua might be hanging out.

It's getting late, and I'm hungry. I get a call from my wife, Nancy, who tells me she's at the back ramp of the police department. She wants to know how the investigation is going and how long I'm going to be. I tell her I'm coming down to talk to her. When I get there, she's in the SUV, and my stepdaughter, Icelia, is with her. Nancy says they're on their way to eat, and afterwards she's going to visit her mother.

I don't get into detail with her. I just tell her I'm going to be here for a while and not to wait up. She doesn't like it, but understands. She's been there many times, waiting for me to come home. Sometimes, we forget how much these investigations affect our families. Nancy leaves, and I go back upstairs. We order pizza because all of us are hungry. Once we're finished with the research and the pizza, we hand out copies of Joshua Neuser's file, including his picture. Assignments are handed out to the other detectives. Mike and I decide to check his mother's house.

Cynthia Neuser lives on North Forgeus Avenue. We arrive there and knock on the door. Mr. Neuser answers and, even though we have his picture, I ask him if he is Joshua Neuser. After he confirms that he is, we introduce ourselves. I tell him we're conducting an investigation and feel he might have some information concerning it. I say we need to speak to him. He's curious and agrees to do the interview at the police station. His mother is home, and Joshua tells her he's going to the police station. Ofc. Stobbs then transports him to the main station.

Joshua is placed in one of the video-recorded interview rooms. Mike and I conduct the interview. Joshua appears nervous and unsure of what the investigation is about. I begin the interview by asking him some general questions. I then read him his Miranda rights. He states that he understands them and will answer our questions.

Initially, he tells us that he has been living with his mother since 10/06, and before that he was living on the streets. He says he also lived with a friend by the name of Erik George, who lives on East Edison. He says he uses heroin and drinks alcohol. He says that the last time he used heroin was about a week ago, and the last time he drank was three days ago. We ask if he understands the questions, and if he is feeling the effects of the heroin or alcohol. He says he's coherent and understands the questions.

He's asked about the people he knows and associates with. He mentions the names of Sandy Glazier, Erik George, another person by the name of "Chris," and "Chris's" girlfriend. He can't remember "Chris's" last name or the name of his girlfriend.

He says he met "Chris" at Fry's at 1st/Grant through Sandy. He says two brothers were also there, and he remembers one of them having a prosthetic arm. He says that, about four months ago, "Chris" and his girlfriend were looking for someone to rent a storage unit. He says they didn't have any identification and offered fifty dollars to anyone with ID who would rent it for them. Joshua says he needed the money (for drugs), so he volunteered to rent it for them.

He says that, after he agreed to rent it, he went with the two brothers over to the rental unit. He says that "Chris" and his girlfriend drove together in their own car and met them at the U-Store-It business. He says that, once they arrived, "Chris" went inside with them while his girlfriend waited in the car. He says that "Chris" also bought a lock for the unit from the guy who rented them the storage unit. After the paperwork was finished, they walked over to the unit and looked inside. "Chris" locked it up once they saw that it was empty.

Joshua started receiving bills for the storage locker. He says at first he ignored them, but later he did tell the management that the unit was not his. He says that last December (2006) he tried to get them to take his name off the lease, but they wouldn't do it. He says they wanted him to pay for the unit. He never paid them and left.

He's asked about the phone number he listed on the application: 551-5176. He says that cell phone number belonged to "Chris," and that "Chris" wanted it on the lease. He says that, at one point, he ran into "Chris's" girlfriend at Fry's. He told her the storage unit management wanted him to pay the bill, and they kept on sending him the bill. She told him she would go over and change the name on the unit.

Joshua then asks us about the storage unit, and why we're so interested in "Chris" and his girlfriend. Instead of answering right away, we ask him if he knows what was stored in the unit. He guesses it was probably drugs. He says he never stored anything in the unit and never knew what "Chris" had inside the unit.

Joshua is asked if "Chris" and his girlfriend had any kids. He says he thinks so because there was a car seat in the car they were driving. He says he never saw the kids, but thought they had a couple of them. He says that, at one point, the girlfriend told him they lived in the area of Stone/Ft. Lowell, near the Circle K.

He's asked about Sandy Glazier, and he says she's someone he's known for about three years. He says she's also a heroin addict, and he hangs out with her. He tells us we could probably find Sandy over behind a house in the area of 1st/Grant, because she sleeps there. We then decide to stop the interview to try and find Sandy. We keep Joshua in the holding cell while we go to look for Sandy. Ofc. Stobbs says he's familiar with Sandy and possibly knows where she is.

Day 2: Monday, February 19, 2007

Sunday has now turned into Monday, and at 0030 hours we drive to the area of 1st/Grant and find Sandy Glazier in the back yard of a house on North 1st Avenue. She's advised that we're conducting an investigation and asked if she would be willing to speak with us about it. She agrees and is transported to the police station by Ofc. Stobbs. Once we arrive, she's placed in the other interview room. Mike and I conduct the interview with Sandy.

She's asked general questions and says she mainly lives on the streets, but does have a mailing address on North Castro. She has a landscaping job and hangs out with various people at 1st/Grant. After answering other questions, she's asked about Joshua. She says she's known him for about four years and that he's a heroin junkie, just like she is.

She's asked if she knows "Chris" and his girlfriend. She says she does, and that "Chris" hangs out at the Labor Ready. She says he likes this girl by the name of Samantha. She says Samantha has a boyfriend by the name of "John," and they live in an apartment at Park/Grant. She says Joshua does know "Chris," but is not sure if he knows Samantha.

She says she and Josh know the "Hook and Crook" brothers (Gene and Terry), and they live in a trailer park at Wetmore/

Roger. She says she's not sure if Josh knows where they live. She says they're also heroin addicts. She says she has never introduced them to Josh, but thinks they probably have met in the streets.

She says she wasn't aware that Josh had rented a storage unit and doesn't know why he would, because he doesn't have anything to put in there. She says she doesn't know anything about anyone asking Josh to rent a storage unit. She says she knows Josh shot up (heroin) earlier in the day, and that every day he panhandles to get money for his heroin habit.

She says that, due to a recent major heroin bust (Sinaloa bust), everyone started hanging out together because it was now hard to get heroin, and the streets were dried up. She's asked if she knows of anyone who might know where the two brothers (Hook and Crook) live. She says that John Allen Bryan, a guy currently in custody at the Pima County Jail, would know where they live. She also says the two brothers drive a blue Nissan pickup truck.

At this time, we decide to take a break, and then speak with Joshua again to confront him with Sandy's statement.

We confront Joshua about the inconsistencies in his statement. He is adamant about "Chris" and his girlfriend being the ones who came to him about renting the storage unit for them. He describes "Chris" as a skinny white male with tattoos. He says he did meet the brothers (Hook and Crook) and "Chris" on the streets. He says that "Chris" is also a drug dealer who slings heroin.

He admits he used heroin earlier in the day, but says he's co-herent and understands what he's saying. He says he's still not sure where the two brothers live. He again states that "Chris" is the one who solicited him to rent the storage unit. He says he did it because he needed the money to buy heroin.

We decide to tell Joshua what was found in the storage unit. Mike tells him a dead child was found in the storage unit he rented. Joshua's immediate response is shock and disbelief. He's again asked about "Chris." He says "Chris" and his girlfriend were selling dope, and "Chris" had a Mexican connection.

He says they were driving a silver or gray car with front end damage. He says he still can't remember the girlfriend's name, but describes her as a Mexican girl with long, straight hair. Joshua still says that "Chris" was the one who wanted him to rent the storage unit. Joshua is "freaked out" and keeps saying he can't believe this is happening. He says he doesn't know anything about what was inside the storage unit. At this time, we decide to take a break.

During the break, Joshua knows that Sandy is in the other holding room. They begin talking to one another by yelling back and forth. The holding rooms are close to each other and, if you're in one of the rooms, you can hear when someone is being placed in the other room. Joshua tells Sandy that "Chris" and his girlfriend have killed their kid, and that a dead child was found in the storage unit. He tells her he can't remember "Chris's" name and keeps asking her if she can remember it. She tells him to keep cool, that everything will work out.

We go back and speak with Sandy. She says she does know a drug dealer by the name of "Chris" who does have a girlfriend. She says she doesn't know his last name and can't remember the girlfriend's name. She's asked if "Chris" and his girlfriend have any kids. She says they might have a two-year-old little boy. She says they drove around in a silver/gray car, or possibly a gold Chrysler, with a car seat inside.

She provides a list of associates who might possibly know "Chris" and his girlfriend, including Samantha Droznenk, who is possibly with "Chris." The following is a list of names or associates that she provides:

Michelle Wertman	Samantha Droznenk
Terry Coombs (Crook)	Jonathan Groom
Charles Coombs (Hook)	Chris Groat

Once we have all the information we can get from Sandy and Joshua, we release them and allow them to go home. We know where we can find them if we need to talk to them again. This is a possibility, because we know they'll be reaching out and asking questions in their own drug-related world.

Our analyst at the time, Roxanne Stead, comes to work to assist us in the investigation. She researches all the names and has them prepared and ready for us.

It's getting late, and we decide to go home and get some sleep. By the time we leave, everyone else has checked back in at the police station. All of the information they have is piled up on my desk for review. It's our day off, and we tell Sgt. Valdez we need to continue with the follow-up work. Mike and I are told to come back later in the morning. Mike and I know we're not going to get too much sleep because of the work involved.

I go home and try to sleep. Nancy, lying next to me, senses my restlessness. She tries to relax me as much as possible. I know what we're up against and think to myself, *Who is this little girl, and why did this happen to her?* Eventually, I fall asleep. On numerous occasions, I have needed a hard drink at night to relax and get to sleep. Usually, one drink will do it.

I'm up early and call Mike. We decide to meet at the OME Office. The autopsy is scheduled for 10:00 a.m. Dr. Peters performs the autopsy. It's done rather quickly because the internal organs have liquefied and decomposed to the point where nothing is left except skin, hair, and bones. He says that more studies are going to be needed on the remains.

He says he doesn't notice any visible trauma and, for now, the cause of death is unknown. Dr. Peters says he's going to have the OME anthropologist, Dr. Anderson, take the body and work with it to see if he can determine if there are any injuries. I ask for hair samples for possible DNA. He pulls two sample groups from different areas. These are placed into separate envelopes and into property as evidence. They are labeled as:

#12-MPO- Hair samples

#12.01-MPO-Hair samples

As with any evidence that is collected and moved or transferred, there has to be documentation on who received what from whom. This is called a chain of custody, and one is done when I collect the hair from Dr. Peters. He says that, from here, he will consult with Dr. Bruce Anderson.

After the autopsy, Mike and I head back to the office. I check the messages on my phone and desk. Sandy Glazier left a phone message, and Officer Stobbs left a note saying that Charles and Terry Combs possibly live at a trailer complex on North 4th Avenue, Space #58.

We decide to check it out and drive over there. We find the trailer and speak to the tenant. He tells us the Coombs brothers no longer live there. They've moved to the Santa Clara Apartments. He tells us they drive a small, bluish/teal-colored pickup truck.

We go over to the Santa Clara Apartments on South Santa Clara. While we're on the way there, Mike receives a call from Lt. Hovden, who tells Mike that the Commanders want us back at the office to update them on the investigation. Mike informs me of the meeting. I look at him and nothing needs to be said. He and I are in agreement. He calls Lt. Hovden and tells him we've located some witnesses and that, for now, we cannot respond back to the office.

We do tell him, however, that we'll go and meet with them as soon as we have spoken to the possible witnesses. I understand why they need to be given updates during the course of the investigation, but sometimes it has to wait.

Lt. Hovden understands and says he'll advise Capt. Richards, Assistant Chief Roberto Villasenor (now Chief of Police at TPD), and the other commanders, but he wants us immediately back at the office as soon as we're done.

I sense even more stress, because now this has become a high profile case, and the department wants answers as quickly as we get them. I know I just need to stay focused on the investigation and try not to worry about the politics and the media attention that is picking up. Mike assures me we'll find out who the little girl is and what happened to her.

Once we arrive at the apartment complex, we drive around until we find the truck we think is the one the tenant described to us. Mike runs the plate, and it's registered to one of the Coombs brothers at the same address and apartment number. We go to their apartment and knock on the door. They are actually home.

We introduce ourselves, and they let us in. We tell them we're conducting an investigation that they might have information about. They are basically cooperative, and we begin to ask them questions about "Chris" and his girlfriend. One of the brothers is not paying too much attention because he's watching a segment of the Three Stooges on TV.

They do say they have no knowledge of "Chris" or his girlfriend. We show them a photograph of Samantha Droznenk from the research that was done. They recognize Samantha's photo and say she's with a guy named "John," not "Chris," and lives in an apartment complex in the area of Park/Grant, Apartment #10. Our intention is to go to the apartment and speak with Samantha, but first we have a meeting to attend.

We brief with the commanders, Police Information Officer (PIO) Lt. George Rodriguez, Capt. Richards, and Lt Hovden. They're provided with the updated information. By now, the media is all over the case and wants information. The PIO is advised of the investigation and initially puts out general information on the case to the media. We try to keep the information as general and simple as possible, so we can focus on what we're doing and not worry about interference from the media.

At the meeting, I advise the commanders that we're probably going to get requests from other agencies to look at their cases on missing children. I tell them that, at this time, I don't want to look at any reports or requests from any outside agencies. But I tell them we need to keep a file on those requests, with an assigned detective to receive them and keep them on file to work them if it comes down to that.

We also need to set up a tip line and have the same detective work that, too. I tell them that, for now, I want to focus on this case and keep it in the Tucson area. Once it appears that it didn't happen here, or we run out of leads, then we can expand the investigation beyond our jurisdiction. I tell them to let us see where this takes us and let us see what we come up with first. They're okay with that, and we move on.

After the meeting, we respond to apartment #10 on North Park. Samantha Droznenk and Jonathan Groom are at home and agree to be interviewed. They're transported to the main station for the interviews and are placed in the holding cells. They're spoken to individually, and I read them their Miranda rights. Both of them say they understand and are willing to speak to us.

Jonathan says a friend named "Chris" was "hot" for his girlfriend. He says that the "Chris" he's talking about worked at McDonalds. Apparently, this "Chris" is not the person we're looking for. Jonathan doesn't too have much more information to offer besides that. Samantha is also questioned, and she gives us the same basic information. She also doesn't have too much to offer. Neither of them knows of any other persons named "Chris" or his girlfriend.

We decide we're going to ask for buccal samples from everyone we bring into the Police Department for questioning. We want to make sure we don't let the parents slip by. Jonathan and Samantha agree to provide buccal samples for DNA.

A buccal sample is taken with a sterile package of extended Q-Tips. Each package contains a set of two Q-Tips. You swab inside the mouth of each inner cheek and place the Q-Tips in a sealed package. You have to wear latex gloves to eliminate cross-contamination of the Q-tips with your own DNA. These samples are now taken and placed into evidence as:

#13-MPO-1 set of buccal swabs from Samantha Droznenk
#14-MPO-1-set of buccal swabs from Jonathan Groom

Jonathan and Samantha are eliminated as persons of interest.

Day 3: Tuesday, February 20, 2007

When I arrive at work, I start going through my messages. I'm beginning to get requests from other agencies to look into their missing children reports. I've also received a call from the National Center for Missing and Exploited Children. I advise them to send me their paperwork and information so I can have it on hand in case I need it. The FBI also offers their assistance. I keep them in mind and take the agent's number.

As the investigation continues, there are more media requests for information. Capt. Richards starts handling the media release statements. By now, the media coverage has expanded, and this story actually goes nationwide for a short time via CNN, I believe. I speak to Carlos about setting up the tip line and keeping the other agency file going. He assigns a detective who is on light duty to handle this.

Cynthia Neuser calls me and informs me she's spoken with Joshua about the case. She says that together they went over all the information they could remember. She says they might have some more information for us. Det. Walker and I go over to her house and speak with her. She says Josh told her about his involvement in the investigation. She says she wants to help in any way possible because Josh told her we're investigating the death of a child whose body was found in the storage unit. She says Joshua is not home right now, but will be back later that day.

She says that, when she spoke to Joshua, he described "Chris" to her and stated that "Chris" lived in the Ft. Lowell/Stone area. She says that "Hook and Crook" (Charles and Terry Combs) know "Chris." She also says she knows a guy by the name of "Zack," who at one time lived with "Chris" and a female named "Reina." She says she thinks that "Zack's" parents live on East Hampton. We don't record the conversation because this is all she has, but we write down the names she gives us. I tell her we'll be back later to talk to Joshua.

Pieces of the investigation are starting to come together and we now have an idea of who "Chris and Reina" are and where they might be living. Mike and I feel that this is the beginning of getting to them.

Later in the day, Joshua calls me and tells me that on 02/19/07 he saw "Reina" at the Fry's at 1st/Grant. He says he approached her and began asking her some questions. He says she ignored him and told him she didn't know what he was talking about. He says she got into her car to leave and, as she was leaving, he wrote down the license plate to her car: 101WGB.

We then conduct the research on the plate and decide to set up surveillance on the address listed on the registration. The vehicle is seen at an apartment complex and, after a short time, we see two women get into the car and drive off.

As Mike and I are following the car, he calls for a uniformed officer in the area to conduct a traffic stop. While we're waiting for the patrol unit to respond to the area, a patrol sergeant, now retired, wants to know which unit is requesting the stop. Mike is driving, so I get on the air and advise the Sergeant to go over to the cross-talk channel. He doesn't do this at first and orders the uniformed officers not to conduct the stop until they have a reason why it's needed. Mike tells him it's in reference to a 0101, which means a homicide.

TPD uses numerous radio frequencies or channels. Officers use the cross-talk channel when they want to bypass the dispatcher while talking with other officers. You would advise the officer to go to that frequency to talk about tactics or to give that person information on what you need. That way, you don't tie up the radio on the normal channels just to pass on information.

The sergeant moves over to the cross-talk channel and, as I'm trying to explain our situation to him, a uniformed officer is across the street, coming out of the cemetery in front of us. Mike is on the regular frequency and asks him to conduct the stop. The officer stops the car, and we're behind them in our unmarked car.

I ignore the sergeant I'm still connected to on the cross-talk channel. To me, following up on the stop is a little more important than trying to explain to him why we've requested the stop. I figure I can speak to him later about it, but for now we need to talk to the occupants in the car. The sergeant that I've basically ignored is extremely butt hurt over what's happening. We don't find out how upset until later.

We approach the two occupants and introduce ourselves. They identify themselves as Maria Orona and Sonya Perez. We advise them that we're conducting an investigation and ask if they would be willing to speak with us. They agree to conduct an interview and voluntarily drive in their own car down to the main police station.

As we're leaving, the force commander of the day arrives and wants to speak with me. The Captain, whom I've known and worked for, wants to know why we requested the stop. I tell him why we needed the car stopped, and why it was important to identify the occupants. I tell him this could be tied to a possible homicide, and we need to get an interview from them. I tell him we didn't mean to ignore the sergeant, but this is a priority.

He sort of smiles and says that next time I should try to advise them of the stop a little sooner. Mike and I leave, and I tell him what the Captain said. Mike can't believe the sergeant wouldn't authorize the stop. I know the sergeant and, in my opinion, he's always had an enormous ego. It doesn't bother me one bit that he was butt hurt over this. In fact, I kind of enjoy it.

After that, we respond to the station. Not until later do I find out that the sergeant complained to my boss and our lieutenant. Rumor has it that our lieutenant chewed him out and told him that what Mike and I were doing was a priority, and if we ever needed to conduct any other traffic stops not to question it. I'm not sure whether this actually took place or not, I don't know, but I heard it from a good source.

When we arrive at the station, we conduct the interviews with the occupants of the car. Maria, the driver, states that on 02/19/07 she was in the Fry's parking lot (1st/Grant) and was approached by a guy who claimed he knew her. She says she didn't know him and was startled. She says she just wanted to get away from him, so she got into her car and left. Joshua was apparently wrong about this person being Reina.

Sonya is also interviewed, and she says she's a friend of Maria's and was taking her to work. At the conclusion of the interview, it's apparent she doesn't have any important information to offer to the investigation. Maria does agree to provide a buccal sample and is eliminated as a person of interest. This sample is listed as:

#15-MPO 1-set of buccal swabs from Maria Orona

Carlos sets up a briefing at the main station with all of the DCU (Dependent Child Unit) Detectives. He takes up some of our concerns with the commanders and advises them of our needs. He says that Crime Analyst Kathy Martinjak is now assigned to assist us with the case until she's no longer needed. Det. Lonnie Bynum from the Counter Narcotics Alliance is also called in to assist. Lonnie has worked narcotics for more than fifteen years and is a top narcotics guy. If anyone would know these players, he would.

Lonnie is asked if he's familiar with any of the first names we've collected. He says he's familiar with some of them and provides us with the following names. He says "Zack" is possibly "Zack

Peterson," and "Kris" (with a "K") is possibly "Kris Houlihan." He also states he's familiar with the "Sinaloa Heroin Ring" and the persons arrested from the sting.

Analyst Martinjak researches these names and other associates. She provides us with the following information. She discloses that Kris bailed "Deb Reyes" out of jail from charges related to the heroin investigation. John Allen Bryan, Zach Peterson, Kris Houlihan, and other names and addresses of possible leads are provided. These leads are then assigned to the detectives working the case.

Detectives Craig Arndt and Lisa Lopez canvas various businesses in the area of 1st/Grant, seeking more information and possible leads. Mike and I decide to put together a couple of photographic line-ups to see if Joshua can pick out Kris. This assignment is given to Calvin Fuller and Sean Holewinski.

Day 4: Wednesday, February 21, 2007

Detectives Holewinski and Calvin Fuller follow up on the leads from the briefing with negative results. They try to find Joshua Neuser at his home to show him the photographic line-ups that have been put together by Det. Walker. Joshua isn't there, so afterwards they try to find Michelle Wertman and Kris Houlihan, also with negative results.

Detectives Arndt and Lopez are assigned to conduct an interview with John Bryan, who's in custody at the Pima County Jail for narcotic offenses. After responding there, they conduct an interview with him. He provides them with the names of Patrick Lane and Sandra Olberg, who he says may possibly have information on "Chris and Reina."

While the detectives are working their assignments, Mike and I decide to take some of the insect evidence collected from the Rubbermaid tub and Hilfiger bag to OME. We meet with Dr. Bruce Anderson and tell him we're investigating the case of the child found in the storage unit. He tells us he did examine the child's remains and discovered that the child had sustained 11 anterior and posterior broken ribs, with injuries to the right forearm and jaw. He states that the broken ribs were chronic (not recent) and were at a healing stage.

He explained it as follows: When a bone is broken, the body begins to heal by reinforcing itself with calcium deposits that build on top of a layered membrane on the bone. This is called the periosteum. This healing process develops as a cluster of calcium over the broken bone and will show up on an x-ray as a white cluster. When the bone has had sufficient amount of time to heal, the cluster remodels itself and eventually forms into the bone itself, leaving very little trace of a broken bone. The developmental stages may vary depending on the amount of time the bone has had to heal.

In this case, Dr. Anderson estimates that the healing fractures are at least six weeks old, due to the amount of calcium on the bone. He also states that the injuries to the jaw and forearm are consistent with someone grabbing them with a hand and squeezing. A rough edge on the jawbone is detected and a bone spur is seen on the forearm. Dr. Anderson says he's not finished and will continue his study of the child's remains.

We tell Dr. Anderson we've brought some of the insects we collected at the scene. He tells us this isn't his area of expertise, and we should consult with Professor Carl Olsen, a University of Arizona entomologist, to get his professional opinion. He says Professor Olsen will probably be a better source of information and will probably be familiar with the collected insects, or will at least have the resources to identify them.

We then speak to Dr. Peters, who tells us that, after consulting with Dr. Anderson and finding out about the child's injuries, he's classifying this death as a "Homicide by Unclear Etiology," which, commonly stated, is "Death by unknown cause."

Day 5: Thursday, February 22, 2007

Analyst Martinjak relays information that she has received from the wiretaps of the Sinaloa Heroin sting. The information we get is that "Deb" is possibly Debbie Reyes, who is currently in the Pima County Jail for narcotic offenses.

Mike and I read her file and respond to the Pima County Jail to conduct an interview with Debra Reyes. We introduce ourselves, and I explain to her that we're conducting an independent investigation unconnected to her case and have no interest in her charges. She looks perplexed, and I tell her again that we're not interested in her current charges or crime.

She's curious and asks us what we're investigating. We initially tell her our investigation involves persons by the names of "Chris and Reina." She tells us she does know them and provides the names of "Chris Payne" and "Reina Gonzales." She says she knows Chris more than Reina, and that Chris Payne is a heroin dealer.

She becomes hesitant to provide us with more information and wants to know what we're investigating. Mike just tells her we're investigating a death. After hearing this, she appears to be more at ease and states that Chris is one of the reasons why she's in jail. She loosens up and is now very cooperative. We don't ask her anything pertaining to that comment.

She then tells us that Chris and Reina used to live at 1702 West 36th Street (Portofino Apartments) in an upstairs apartment, but she's not sure of the apartment number. She's then asked if Chris or Reina have any children. At first, she only recalls them having a little boy with them and says she believes he's their child. She later recalls that, at one time, she saw them with a little girl and thought her name was possibly "Ashley."

She's then asked if she would be willing to provide a buccal sample for DNA. I tell her we need it to eliminate her as a possible suspect in the death investigation. She agrees, and the sample is taken. This is listed as:

#16 MPO-1-set of buccal swabs from Deborah Reyes.

It's getting late in the afternoon, and Mike and I are exhausted. I can only speak for myself, but every night since the investigation started, I have not slept very well. The case is constantly on my mind, and I keep going over and over what needs to be done. I also see in my mind the remains of the little girl and sense the smell of death. I keep asking myself the questions, "Who are you, and who did this to you?" I try to picture the little girl that she was—laughing, playing, being a normal child. I think to myself that the type of evil person who is really capable of doing this has no soul and is truly going to hell. I know that, inside, I'm driven to find the person or persons responsible for doing this. I also know that Mike feels the same way I do. I'm glad we're paired up on this one.

Mike and I decide to respond to 1702 West 36th Street and speak with the management. Renda Alvarado is the manager, and Ana Ontiveros is the assistant manager. They confirm that Chris Payne and Reina Gonzales lived in Apt. #2109 until August 2006. They provide us with copies of the lease information they have on file. We don't check the apartment at this time and don't ask if someone has since moved in because it's been such a long time since Chris and Reina left.

It's now late afternoon, and we're tired. We decide to go home.

Day 9: Monday, February 26, 2007

We meet with Analyst Kathy Martinjak and give her the information on the lease. She researches the names of "Chris" and "Reina" and comes up with the names of family members and associates. This information is dispersed for follow-up with the other detectives.

In the meantime, the pile of information is collecting on my desk. I sort through it and try to keep it organized as much as I can. My desk is in the form of controlled chaos. I do keep it sorted out. I start making a "to do" list for each day and prioritize the entries.

I have to make time to meet Crime Lab DNA Analyst Nora Rankin. I sit down with her and ask her what needs to be collected from the child's remains for obtaining a DNA profile. She tells me I need to collect a molar, a long bone sample, and a rib sample.

I call Dr. Anderson and advise him of what I need from the remains of the child. I tell him this is for our lab, so we can have the samples tested to obtain a DNA profile. He says he'll get the samples ready for me. After a while, I go to the OME office and meet with Dr. Anderson. He gives me the requested samples. The following is a list of the collected items:

#17MPO:
1-Tooth "I", maxillary left first (deciduous molar)
1-Tooth "S" mandibular right first (deciduous molar)
1-osseous sample of the second left rib
1-osseous sample of the right femur
1-osseous sample from the left tibia

I'm also informed that a small rock from the sacral area and a plastic/cloth fragment were found on the child's body. After signing the chain of custody form, I take these items and place them into property as evidence. The rock does not prove to be an item of evidentiary value.

I meet with Nora and advise her of the collected samples from OME. She tells me that the samples I've received need to be sent to an outside lab to extract the DNA for a profile. She says that, once a DNA profile is established, she'll be able to use it for her analysis on any of the collected DNA evidence. She recommends that the samples be sent to the University of North Texas Health Science Center at Ft. Worth, and says she'll make the arrangements.

During the time I was researching the collection of the DNA evidence and responding to OME, Mike took the information we had on "Reina" and "Chris" and developed photographic line-ups on each of them. Our intention is to see if they can be identified in a line-up to ensure this is the same Chris we're talking about.

We respond to the Pima County Jail and again meet with Deborah Reyes. We show her the photographic line-ups of Christopher Payne and Reina Gonzales. She looks at them and picks Reina Gonzales out of the line-up. She then looks at Christopher Payne's line-up and initially picks him out. She does, however, state that there's one other individual in the line-up who also looks like Chris. She says it's been awhile since she last saw him.

After that, we go over to Ms. Neuser's home to speak with Joshua again. We find Joshua at home and show him the same facial line-ups of Chris Payne and Reina Gonzales. After viewing them, he states that it's been a while since he last saw them and thinks their looks have changed from the photographs we have. He isn't sure, but he does take a guess on whom they might be in the line-up. He never picks them out, but it's not surprising. After all, he's addicted to heroin and is barely functional.

Joshua tells us that, during the weekend, he was out looking for Reina. He says he did find out that Reina's mother, "Jenny," lives in an apartment on West Alturas. We ask him if he's willing to provide us a set of buccal samples. He agrees to it and, after obtaining the sample, I place it into property as evidence, listed as item:

#18MPO-1-set of buccal swabs from Joshua Neuser.

We then go to Kino Abraham Health Center Vital Records and attempt to obtain birth records on any possible children that Chris Payne and Reina Gonzales might have. The local office refers us to Doug Leach (supervisor) in Phoenix. Mike speaks to him and advises him of the investigation.

Mr. Leach says he needs to do some research and will call back. He calls Mike back and tells him there's no current record of "Chris" having any children under his name, but does state that Reina is listed as having only one child. We're a little confused by the fact that only one child is listed.

We then respond to the East Alturas Apt #F address and speak with Jenny Gonzales (Reina's mother). We introduce ourselves and advise her that we need to speak with her in regard to an investigation. She states she hasn't seen Reina in a while and confirms that Chris Payne is Reina's boyfriend. She tells us she thinks Reina is possibly working at the Golden Corral on 22nd Street/Columbus Avenue. We do not record the conversation.

I did notice that Jenny has a black eye and was nervous about speaking with us. I don't trust her or believe that she hasn't seen or heard from Reina in a while. We could tell that Jenny has lived a rough life. She's somewhat obese and looks like she has consistently used drugs the past. It's probably safe to say, from the shiner on her eye, that she has a boyfriend who took it to her.

Mike and I drive over to the Golden Corral restaurant at 22nd Street/Columbus, where we speak to the manager, Keith Brogdon. We ask him about Reina and if she's still employed there. He pulls her work file and states that Reina was fired on 02/04/07 for not showing up. He gives us a copy of her file and provides us with her last known address on North Stone Avenue. In her file and application, she listed three names as references. The listed names are Mirna Gonzales, Regina Munoz, and Matt Ovato. We do not record the interview.

Mike and I decide to respond to the North Stone Avenue address. We look for a manager and are told by some of the tenants that there is no on-site manager. They say we can call management and give us the number. Mike makes the call and speaks to a representative. He's told that Chris and Reina moved in on August/06 and were evicted for non-payment of rent in January/07.

He's told that the couple had only one child listed on the lease. They moved right away and left all of their belongings behind. The management said they disposed of their property after sending out a notification letter warning of intent to dispose of their property.

Mike and I then meet with the beat officer, Ofc. Tom Rizzi, and advise him of the investigation. We tell him we need to speak to a Christopher Payne and Reina Gonzales and show him photographs of the two of them. He says he's not familiar with them, but does say he'll contact us if he finds them.

Shortly after we leave, Ofc. Rizzi informs us over the radio that a 9-1-1 call has just come in from the pay phones at the Circle K at 1st/Glenn. Someone left a message saying they have information that "Chris and Regan" put the body of the missing girl in the storage locker. Ofc. Rizzi responded to the Circle K, but the caller apparently left before he arrived. One of the store employees says she thought that someone at the pay phones left in a white Chevy Suburban with blue stripes. Mike and I canvass the area, but do not locate the Suburban.

We then respond back to the Circle K and meet with the store employees and Ofc. Rizzi. Mike speaks to the employees and attempts to get a copy of the video. It's not available at this time, so Mike says he'll come back the next day to get it.

Day 10: Tuesday, February 27, 2007

Mike responds back to Circle K and obtains the videotape. Ms. Martinjak provides us with more packets of information about Reina and her work records. It appears that the information from one of the packets resembles a female relative of Reina (Marisela Gonzales) whom we suspect made the call from the Circle K.

Mike and I respond to an address on West Helton to speak with Marisela Gonzales. We knock on the door, and her teenage kids tell us she's not home, but working at Jack In The Box, 6th/44th Street. We drive to her work and see her cleaning the tables. We introduce ourselves and advise her of an investigation involving "Reina" and "Chris." She agrees to talk and tells us that Reina is her cousin, and she's not seen her in over a year.

She says she knows that Chris Payne is Reina's boyfriend, and he has two kids from a previous marriage. She states that Chris pays child support on the kids, and this has been a sore spot for Reina, because most of the money she earns goes toward the child support. She says she doesn't know where they now live. This is basically all the information she has to offer. We just speak to her and do not record the interview. We are unable to confirm whether Marisela was the person who made the 9-1-1 call at the Circle K.

Mike works off-duty at the local DES (Department of Economic Security) every Thursday and says he can get more information on Chris and Reina. We respond to DES Child Support office, and Mike asks them to research Christopher Payne and Reina Gonzales. They tell us they can't find Christopher in the system. They do advise that on 12/10/06, Reina Gonzales applied for assistance for Ariana, Tyler, and Chris, Jr. There is no record of the dates of birth for these children or any other information on them. We leave and head back to the office.

While Mike is driving, I place a call to the Child Support Division at Superior Court. I identify myself and ask the clerk to research Christopher Payne and Reina Gonzales. They confirm that Christopher Payne has two children and identify them as Tyler and Ariana Payne. They also tell me that Jamie Hallam is the mother of these children, and that Chris Payne is over $19,000 in arrears in child support payments to her. They state they have no other listed information on the children or Jamie Hallam. I suggest to Mike that maybe Chris doesn't want to pay the child support, and this was his motive for killing the children.

They do advise that, in January of 2007, they did try to garnish wages from Mr. Payne's previously listed employer at SKOR, but were unsuccessful. SKOR is a transportation service that drives the disabled and elderly to their medical appointments.

As we're driving back to the office, a cold chill comes over me. I turn to Mike and tell him I believe our victim is Ariana Payne. What I don't understand is the fact that this is the first time we've ever heard of Tyler. I tell Mike that if our victim is Ariana, then where is Tyler? I also tell him that if Ariana were killed or murdered, then what would stop them from killing Tyler? I tell him if they could kill one child, they could kill the other one, too.

Mike agrees it's possible, but says we need to do the research on the kids before we jump to conclusions. My mind is racing, and I'm anxious to get back to the office to research the information and see what it reveals. He knows I'm bothered by this and tells me to settle down, to take it one step at a time. This is why it's so great to work with Mike. He always keeps everything in check, advises me on what's important at the time, and reminds me not to get overzealous.

When we arrive back at the office, I call Sgt. Valdez to update him on the information. He says to just sit on the information for now until we can confirm what we have. It's late in the evening. Mike decides to go home to his family. I stay at the office and decide to call CPS (Child Protective Services) to see if there's a possible history on the family.

I speak with Olivia Bartfalvi and ask her to research the names of Christopher Payne and Jamie Hallam. She advises me that they're in the system, and there's a CPS history on both of them. She says Jamie is a suspected "meth" user. She continues with the information and tells me that Chris and Jamie do have two children, Tyler and Ariana Payne. She tells me that Tyler was born on 11/15/01. Ariana's date of birth is 10/18/02, and she describes Ariana as having reddish-brown hair.

Ms. Bartfalvi goes on to tell me that Chris was allowed to keep the children because of Jamie's suspected drug use. She says that in December/06 Jamie had another baby and was investigated for drug use because the baby tested positive for having amphetamines in her system. She says there was also a report listed where Jamie called TPD in March/06, asking for assistance to find her kids and for help in the custodial issue between her and Chris.

At that time, Christopher Payne displayed documentation to the officer, showing that he was trying to gain custody of the children. The officer apparently contacted CPS, who advised him to allow the children to stay with Mr. Payne. Ms. Bartfalvi gives me the last known addresses for Jamie. She is listed as living in Catalina on North Twin Lakes Drive and on East Tortolita Street. At my request, Ms. Bartfalvi forwards all of the CPS reports over to me.

Calvin Fuller is one of my colleagues in the unit. He is still in the office when I make the call to CPS. After receiving the information from CPS, I get goose bumps, and a cold chill once again comes over me. I turn to Cal and tell him I believe I just found out who our victim is. She fits the physical description, and the age matches up. But I'm still not sure about Tyler or his whereabouts. Cal says it seems like a possibility.

At some point, Cal goes home, though I don't notice when he leaves. I'm the only one in the office, and I need to get this information. I then begin to receive the paperwork from CPS through the fax machine. As I'm receiving it, I realize I'm getting redacted copies. All of the personal information has been blacked out, including addresses and dates of birth verifying what I know. I call Ms. Bartfalvi back and tell her I need the un-redacted CPS copies. She tells me that the records supervisor advised her that I was not entitled to the un-redacted copies. I become angry and tell her I am entitled to them by law, and that I want them immediately.

I realize it's not her fault and ask to speak the person in charge. She gives me the supervisor's phone number, and I speak to the person in charge. She tries to tell me we're not authorized to get un-redacted copies. I become very irate and tell her she doesn't know what she's talking about; according to state law, they're required to share any information they have on an investigation to any law enforcement agency.

I tell her I'm possibly conducting a murder investigation, and that the two children on their reports are unaccounted for and could be the victims. I tell her she had better send me the un-redacted copies immediately, or there will be hell to pay in the morning when I take this issue to a higher authority, who will see it my way. She sends me the un-redacted CPS reports. I usually do not react this way, but there's a lot at stake here, and I'm not in the mood to put up with any preventable glitches.

I call Carlos and advise him of the information I've received. I tell him about the disagreement I had with the CPS Custodian of Records. He tells me not to worry about it; he'll deal with that later. I tell him Mike and I are going to Catalina first thing in the morning to track down Jamie Hallam. Carlos tells me he doesn't want to call any commanders tonight, but he'll advise them in the morning. He says there will probably be a briefing.

After speaking with Carlos, I call Mike and advise him of the information I've received. He agrees to go with me to look for Jamie first thing in the morning.

Before I leave to go home, I decide to read all of the CPS reports, and I pull the TPD incident report from March 2006 and read that. Uniformed officers did respond to Chris's apartment on a possible custodial incident. When the officers conducted the investigation, they were told by CPS to leave the kids with Chris because there was an open CPS report on Jamie.

That officer also documented how Chris told him he was filing for custody of the kids, but hadn't finished the paperwork. The officer checked on the kids, and they seemed at the time to be healthy. After that, CPS did not follow up with the kids to check on them, and Jamie would never hear or see her kids again.

Day 11: Wednesday, February 28, 2007

In the morning, Mike and I attempt to locate Jamie in Catalina, Arizona. We first respond to the address on North Twin Lakes Drive and speak to her stepfather, Richard Barcalow, and other family members. We introduce ourselves and tell them we're investigating the custodial issues involving Jamie, Chris, and their children. They seem to understand and give us some basic information on them. They do state that they haven't seen the kids for a while, and they know Chris has them.

We ask them if they have any current pictures of the kids. They're very cooperative and seem happy that we're involved. They provide us with photographs of the children. I am moved when I see pictures of the kids for the first time. They tell us that Jamie doesn't live with them, but does live nearby on Tortolita Street. They offer to show us where she lives, and one of the sons escorts us over to her house. He tells us that Jamie is home and drives off.

I knock on the door, and several minutes pass before she opens it. We seem to have waited her out, because she finally steps out and greets us. I can only speculate that she doesn't want to talk to us; we're cops, and she hasn't had too many positive contacts with the police. I can tell she's nervous and very standoffish. Mike and I introduce ourselves, and we tell her we're investigating the custodial issues that she has with Chris. We tell her this because, at this time, we're not sure what to think, and we need to get some answers about her kids. I know it's not the complete truth, but we need a reason to talk to her. This reason sounds believable to her, and I can tell she's now more comfortable talking to us.

My first impression of Jamie is that she's a "meth-head." She fits the pattern. She's very thin and pale, with pick marks on her arms and face. She seems to understand why we're there and is cooperative with us. After being asked, she agrees to an audio-recorded interview. She doesn't want us to go into her trailer, so the interview is conducted in my detective car. Jamie sits in the front passenger seat, and Mike is seated behind her in the passenger side of the back seat.

The interview starts out with some general questions. After she answers them, we move towards asking her about the children and the relationship she had with Chris. She says she's divorced from Chris and that together they had Tyler and Ariana. She says the court awarded her full custody of the children. She says that in December 2005 Chris called and requested a visitation with the kids. She allowed the visitation and, after he'd had them for a couple of weekends, she called Chris and told him she wanted the kids back. He brought them back, and later he asked her for another visitation. She said that the last time she saw the kids was January 20, 2006, when she drove the kids over to Chris's place and dropped them off.

She called Chris again and asked to get the kids from him. He kept putting her off, and on February 3, 2006 he stopped communicating with her. When asked if she knows where the kids are, she tells us they're with Chris. I ask her if she has the court-ordered documentation for the children. She says she does and later on provides it to us.

She states that she's been trying to find her kids and has made several reports to the local law enforcement agencies and CPS, trying to get them back. She says that in March 2006 she called TPD and met them at the Portofino Apartments to try and get her kids back. She says the officer met with Chris and saw the kids. The officer told her that Chris was filing a court order to try and gain custody of them. She was told that, when the officer contacted CPS, they told him to allow Chris to keep the kids because of an open on-going investigation they had on her. She has not seen or heard anything about them since then.

I then ask her to describe her children to me. She says Tyler has brown hair, a small freckle on his foot, and speaks with an impediment. Ariana has thin, light brown hair, probably shoulder length, and straight teeth. She says she has pictures of the children.

She says that Chris and Reina no longer live at the Portofino Apartments, and she doesn't know where they currently live. She says that, at one point, she left Chris during their marriage because he started getting into methamphetamines. She denies using any drugs. I ask her if she feels the children are in danger being with Chris. She thinks they are in danger because of his drug problem.

Jamie also tells us that her mother, Linda Cosentino, who lives in New Jersey, spoke to the children over the phone last June. During that conversation, Ariana was crying because her daddy had hit her in the head. Ariana also told Ms. Cosentino that Tyler was sleeping in the bedroom because he was in trouble, too. Jamie provides me with Ms. Cosentino's phone number after I ask her for it.

I explain to Jamie that part of the custodial investigation is that we need proof to determine who the biological parents are. I then ask her for buccal samples for DNA. She's told that the samples are needed for DNA in helping determine the custody of her children. After she agrees, I take the buccal samples. These samples are listed as:

19MPO-1-set of buccal swabs from Jamie Hallam.

These are later placed into property as evidence. She then provides us with photographs of the children. These are added to the ones her stepfather gave us previously.

I know I've lied to Jamie about this, but I need to get her samples to help determine if the child in the storage unit is her daughter, Ariana. After viewing the photographs and knowing Ariana's age, it's apparent that she's close to fitting the description of the remains at OME.

Jamie provides additional information about her family and Chris. She's done her own research and found out that he moved from the Portofino Apartments to an address on North Stone Avenue. We ask other questions, and she answers them. We conclude the interview. I give her my business card with my number. At this point in time, Mike and I are very concerned for Tyler, because there have been no sightings of him or any other information as to where he is. It's like he exists and doesn't exist.

We go back to the office and conduct a briefing with the command staff. They're given an update on the recent information.

Everyone is obviously in agreement that our investigation now needs to focus on finding Chris and Reina. They are the key to finding out what happened to these kids. We're told to use whatever resources we need.

The Hunt

Still Day 11: Wednesday, February 28, 2007

At one point, I'm at the Pima County Attorney's office to discuss another case that needs to be handled. I run into Bunkye Chi, one of the prosecuting attorneys. She asks me how the case is going. I tell her I have a couple of strong leads that I'm focusing on and to be ready when it breaks open. She smiles and says okay.

Ms. Martinjak conducts the research on Chris and Reina and gives us a research packet on each of them. We find out that there's an outstanding misdemeanor warrant on Chris for driving on a suspended license. Utility checks are conducted, and the records from Tucson Electric Power show that Stephanie Gable was listed as a contact when Reina had service at the Los Arboles Apartments. Stephanie Gable's last known address is on East 31st Street. Detectives Arndt and Lopez are given that assignment and respond to that address to speak with her. Instead of finding Stephanie, they discover that it's the home of Mirna Gonzales (Reina's aunt). She's cooperative and gives them a statement.

When they get back, they brief us on Mirna's statement. She told them that Reina came over to her house in January 2007 with her two-year-old son, Christopher Payne, Jr. Reina asked her for money, and Mirna refused to give her any money because she felt she was using drugs.

Mirna said the last address she had for Reina was at the Palm Court Inn, 4425 East 22nd Street. She said that Chris and

Reina were driving a Plymouth Breeze with a missing hood. The detectives obtained other information. That information is given to Ms. Martinjak, who does the research and creates files on the information.

I go over the packets and telephone messages on my desk. Linda Cosentino (Jamie's mother) has called me from New Jersey and left a message asking to speak with me. Apparently, Jamie called her, told her to call me, and gave her my number.

I call her back and explain to her that we're investigating the custodial situation between Chris and Jamie, and we're looking for the children. I ask her when was the last time she spoke to the kids. She says the last time she spoke to them was on May 30, 2006. She says that, when she called, Chris answered the phone. She asked if she could speak to the kids. Chris first put Ariana on the phone. She was happy to be speaking with her. The conversation didn't last too long, but Ariana told her several times that her head hurt, but didn't say why. She then spoke to Tyler, and he basically told her that he got his butt beat. She hung up and was very concerned about the welfare of the children. At one point, she called Pat Payne (Chris's stepmother) in Virginia, and after they spoke to each other they were in agreement that they were concerned for the welfare of the kids.

She also says that, at one time, she did make a call to CPS. She has some other information and gives it to me during the interview. I record what is said. I then tell everyone that we now know that Ariana was alive up until May 30, 2006. Everyone gets quiet for a moment, and then continues what they were doing.

Cal and Sean are given the assignment of conducting interviews with family members related to Chris and Reina. Det. Arndt and Lopez are out in the field. They go to the Palm Court Inn and speak to the management. They're told that Chris and Reina are currently living in apartment #312.

They also find out that Chris, Reina, and Chris, Jr. moved in on 01/11/07 and are the only ones listed on the lease. Cal and Sean drive around the parking lot and see the white Plymouth with the missing hood parked in the north parking lot. They call and tell us they're standing off, conducting surveillance at the Palm Court Inn.

A briefing is held, and it's decided that more assistance is going to be needed for continued surveillance. Sgt. Mike Allen works in the special undercover unit and is contacted. His unit is assigned to assist in the surveillance. Their assignment is to relieve our unit and cover the overnight shift.

At one point, we decide to approach the apartment to see if anyone is there. We knock on the door several times, but no one answers. We then back off, and the surveillance is continued. Sgt. Mike Allen's squad shows up around 10:00 p.m. and takes over for the night. During the course of our surveillance, no activity is seen at the apartment.

Day 12: Thursday, March 1, 2007

In the morning our unit arrives and relieves Sgt. Allen's squad. After no activity, it's decided to have Det. Arndt speak with the Palm Court Inn management. This is around 10:00 a.m. They provide him with information on other possible vehicles that Chris and Reina might be driving. They also advise him that their rent is due on the 1st or 2nd day of the month (March), and that Chris and Reina should be coming in to pay it. They also state they've seen Reina with a child in a stroller.

At about 1100 hours, Reina calls the office and states they'll be in around 5:00 p.m. to pay the rent. A check on the phone number Reina called from is traced to the Lazy 8 Motel, 314 East Benson Highway.

Mike and I immediately break off the surveillance and drive over to the Lazy 8 Motel. We pull up and speak with the management, telling them that we're looking for Chris Payne and Reina Gonzales. They check their registry and confirm that Chris and Reina are in room #106. The management states that their room was rented by Forrest Payne (Christopher Payne's father). As far as they know, Chris and Reina are still in the room.

We then call for the assistance of undercover and uniformed officers to set up a perimeter of containment. From the manager's office, we can see the front door to the room. It's on the bottom floor. We keep it under surveillance and direct the responding units to set up a perimeter, avoiding the front of the apartment complex. Chris and Reina are not about to get away.

Once the perimeter is set up around Lazy 8 Motel, we decide that a call needs to be made by the management. They're asked to place a call to room #106 and tell whoever answers the phone that someone needs to respond to the office to discuss payment on the room.

Mike and I leave and are around the southwest corner of the building, watching and waiting to see who comes out. Reina is the one who steps out, and we immediately approach and stop her. I ask for her name. She tells me she's Reina Gonzales. I see that she's Hispanic, short, thin with long dark hair. I ask her if Chris is with her. At first, she first tells me she doesn't know where he is, but keeps looking towards the room. I see someone looking out between the closed window blinds.

Reina walks with us back to the room and opens the door. Chris is seen inside and is asked to step out. When he does, Mike and I approach him. Officers also surround him, and I ask him for his name. He tells me he's Christopher Payne and wants to know what's going on. Mike and I have been anticipating this moment for some time and are excited to have him in front of us. This is the moment we've been waiting for, and it couldn't have played out any better. I notice that Chris is tall, thin, and has a shaved head with stubble coming in. He doesn't have a shirt on. He does have some tattoos. At this point, he's not in handcuffs, but is detained. I hold back on telling him anything about the investigation involving his kids. It's very important to handle him this way for legal reasons.

I just tell him that we're conducting an investigation, and he might have some information about the case. I ask him if he's willing to go to the police station to discuss the case. He tells me he doesn't want to go anywhere without his attorney.

I then tell him there's an outstanding warrant for him (misdemeanor warrant for driving on a suspended license), and he's under arrest for that warrant. At that point, he's handcuffed and taken into custody. A uniformed officer is assigned to transport him to the Main Police Station.

Uniformed officers are detaining Reina. I go over and take her off to the side, away from everyone. I can see she's upset and wondering why Chris is being taken to jail. I need to put her at ease, so she'll cooperate with us. I tell her he's been arrested on the outstanding warrant, and that's why he's being taken to the police station. She tells me that Chris is her whole life, and she can't function without him. She says she loves him, is lost without him, and doesn't know what to do.

She's very excited, and I have to settle her down. I speak to her very calmly and tell her we're conducting an investigation and believe that she and Chris have information on the case. I ask her if she'll voluntarily go to the main station and speak to us about the investigation. She agrees, but wants to know about her son. I tell her we'll also bring him with us. Uniformed officers then transport her to the main police station.

She and Chris are never told why we want to speak to them or what the investigation is about until they are being interrogated at the police station. Sometimes, you have to keep certain information to yourself, even though the persons involved probably know what it's about. There's always a slight hopeful chance with them that it isn't what they think it is.

Little Chris, Jr. is the only child with Chris and Reina at the Lazy 8 Motel. CPS is notified, and caseworker Cassie Dixon is advised of the situation. She says she'll be responding to the police station to take custody of him, and does so when she arrives. Pima County attorneys Sue Eazer and Bunkye Chi are called and come over to the station. Sue is the Pima County Attorney Supervisor, and Bunkye is one of the prosecuting attorneys in the Violent Crimes Unit. It's apparent that, from this point on, I will be closely working with the two of them on this case.

Chris is put in one of the video-recorded interrogation rooms at the police station. Reina is in the lobby with officers nearby. The interview rooms are being set up with video and audio equipment, and the recording is started. The initial plan is for Mike and I to conduct the interview with Chris, and for me to take the lead on the interview.

The same plan is set up for Reina. The reason we don't place Reina in the interrogation room is because, at this point, we see her more as a witness than a suspect. We're not sure how involved she is or what she knows. We need her to be as comfortable as possible to get her to talk. She's already skittish, and we have to play it this way.

I'm at my desk getting my notes and thoughts together as to how I want to approach Chris to get him to talk. I know this is going to be one of the most important interviews I will ever do as a detective. I want it to go smoothly, but things don't always go as planned, and sometimes you have to deal with the given situation at hand. Mike is also at his desk, and I assume he's doing the same thing.

As we're preparing to interrogate them, one of the detectives tells Mike that Chris is being disorderly in the interrogation room. Mike goes into the room with another officer to try and settle him down. Mike and the officer settle Chris down and, as he's leaving the room, Chris tells Mike he only wants to speak to him, and that he wants to talk right now. Mike tells him we'll be coming in to speak with him soon. He tells Mike that if he leaves now, he won't give a statement. He forces Mike's hand, and Mike stays in the room to conduct the interview with Chris.

I'm not aware of this incident until someone comes over and tells me that Mike is interviewing Chris. At first, I'm annoyed because I don't know the situation. I go over to the viewing area and see a crowd of commanders, detectives, and officers watching. Sue and Bunkye are also there, having arrived after Mike started the interview. I ask Carlos what's happening, and he explains what took place. My ego initially gets the best of me, but as I'm watching the beginning stages of the interview I see that Mike did not deliberately start without me.

I settle down and am relieved that Chris is actually talking to Mike. Sometimes, you have to check your ego at the door and focus on what needs to be done. Sometimes, you have to flow with the situation that's given to you. Mike also later apologizes and wants me to know that he didn't do this on purpose. I tell Mike I'm okay with it, and I'm glad Chris would talk to him.

Mike reads Chris his Miranda rights and, afterward, Chris waives them. After some general questions are asked and answered, Chris becomes somewhat impatient. The flow of the interview is not normal. Chris is erratic. He states he doesn't want to talk anymore unless he can talk to his father, Forrest Payne, or his sister. Mike tells him his dad is on a flight back home, asks who his sister is, and goes with the flow of the interview.

This proves potentially to be a problem with the Miranda rights. Even though Chris did not ask for an attorney, it's a problem, because he now doesn't want to talk to us and has invoked his right to remain silent. I don't think he's doing this intentionally; to me he seems to be doing it to be in control. Whenever it seems like Mike is going to leave or stop the interview, Chris begins talking again and re-initiates the interview. The length of time we have him on video, either talking or just sitting in the interview room, is about five hours.

He then wants to speak about Tyler and Ariana. He tells Mike how much he misses his kids and that they just gave up on him. He blames the kids for not eating while they were under his care and tells how they ate their own feces. He says the kids starved themselves and that he tried to get help, but nobody would help him. He somehow blames Jamie and says that, because of her drug use, he kept the kids in order to protect them. He says he's going to hell for what he did.

He's difficult to interview because he constantly tries to control the situation, and his attention wanders all over the place. His statements are disconnected and lack continuity.

Eventually, he continues on and states that Tyler was with Ariana in the (Tupperware) tub, and they died under his care from starvation at the Portofino Apartments. He states that Ariana died first, and three days to a week later, Tyler died, also from starvation. He says he wrapped Ariana in a black garbage bag, and then placed her in a Hilfiger bag. He then tells Mike that, afterward, he placed her inside the storage unit of their apartment.

He says that, after Tyler died, he placed him in the same type of black garbage bag as Ariana. He then took Ariana out of the tub and placed Tyler at the bottom. Ariana was placed on top of Tyler. He denies physically abusing either Ariana or Tyler.

A briefing with the command staff is conducted regarding the new information on Tyler. It's decided then that a search has to be done into the landfill, and that landfill protocols need to be followed in order to conduct a search for Tyler's remains at the landfill. Calvin is given this assignment and, after the research is done, the driver of the dump truck is found. He's able to isolate the dumpsite area at the Los Reales Landfill, and it's then secured. Officers and detectives search the landfill.

The interview with Chris Payne continues; other questions are asked and answered, and the interview is eventually concluded. I don't observe the entire interview because I leave to speak with Reina, who has been moved into another interview room.

I go into the room and ask her some general questions. Again, she's very curious about why we've brought them to the police station, and why Chris has been arrested. I tell her we'll get to that, and she answers some of my questions. I tell her that, because she's been brought into the police station and is in this room, I need to read the Miranda rights to her, which I do, reading from the rights card. I ask her if she understands and if she will answer my questions. She says she understands and will answer my questions.

I continue asking her general questions and, after she answers them, I move towards asking her about Chris, Ariana, and Tyler. I ask her where they've been living for the past year. She says that recently they were staying at the Lazy 8 Motel, and before that it was the Palm Court Inn, and prior to that it was the apartments on North Stone Avenue. She later says they also lived at the Portofino Apartments.

I ask her what she does for a living. She says she was working as a waitress at Chaffin's restaurant up until two weeks ago. I try to ask her about her immediate family. She's obviously bothered by this and tells me that, at this time, I don't need to talk to her about them. I then ask her about Chris. She says she's known him for about five years. She says that, two weeks after meeting Chris, she moved in with him. She tells me they're not married, but are planning on getting married tomorrow. I wonder if she's thinking about marrying him so she won't be able to testify against him. It wouldn't matter anyway because, in child abuse cases in Arizona, that doesn't apply.

I ask her if she knows his family. She says she does, and that Patricia and Forrest are his stepmom and dad. She says that every year for about two weeks they come down for the Rodeo. She says his parents left this morning, but while they were here she and Chris did get to visit with them. She says Chris's parents helped them financially while they were here.

I ask her why Chris isn't working. She says he does get jobs, but quits after a month or two. She says she's the one who is always working and is under a lot of stress. She says Chris has two kids, Tyler and Ariana (five and three years old) from a previous marriage. I ask her if she knows his ex-wife. She says she's met her and knows who she is.

I ask her if custody or visitations have ever been established through the court system. She says that nothing officially has ever been set. I ask if the kids ever come over for visits, and when was the last time they were there for a visit. She says that sometimes they do come over for visits, and the last time was about a year ago.

I tell her I've spoken with Jamie, and she told me she was concerned about the custodial situation. I again ask Reina when was the last time they had the kids. She says they did have the kids for about two weeks toward the end of last year. She indicates that, during the visit, Jamie came over with her boyfriend and picked them up. She says Chris does not have legal custody, but because of the bad environment the kids were in with Jamie, they just kept them. She says Jamie is into drugs.

I continue to question Reina about the kids, but during the interview she's evasive with her answers and continuously says she can't remember any dates or times, or just gives a general month as a timeline. Her favorite response is, "All I ever do is work, work, and work."

I ask her how many times she's moved within the last six months. She says they've moved three times. She says they've been at the Lazy 8 Motel for one day, were at the Palm Court Inn for three months, and before that they were at the apartments on North Stone Avenue. I ask her if the kids were with them during the time they were at those apartments. She says the last time they had the kids was when they were living at the Portofino Apartments.

I ask her if she knows where the kids are right now. She says she assumes that the kids are with Jamie. She says the kids were with her and Chris for about three weeks until Jamie's boyfriend came over and picked them up.

I ask her how she knows it was Jamie's boyfriend who picked them up (now it's only the boyfriend who picked them up). She says Chris told her that Jamie's boyfriend picked them up while she was at work, because when she came home they were gone.

I ask her if she knows what time they were picked up. She says it was during the day, because she came home from work around 5 or 6 p.m., and the kids were gone. I ask her if she knows what month the kids were picked up. She's evasive, but does say it was in the wintertime. I try to break down the winter months by using reference dates for her (e.g., New Years Eve, Christmas, Thanksgiving, and Halloween). She still claims she can't remember the dates.

I ask her if she knows about the arrangements Chris made with Jamie's boyfriend about picking up the kids. She says she isn't sure who made the plans to have them picked up. She then starts talking about how much time she spends at work and how she doesn't have much time for the family.

I ask her to tell me what Chris is like. She says he's a loving, caring person. I ask her if he ever uses drugs. She says not when they first met. I press her and tell her she needs to be truthful and honest with me. I tell her I want to get to know the both of them, and that's why I need her to be truthful and give me accurate information.

I'm concerned about getting at the truth of this because this may be my only shot at interviewing this suspect. I know it's important to find out what kinds of drugs they were using and how often. Establishing the influence that drugs had on their state of mind during the course of the crimes they committed against the children could be crucial if the case goes to trial. It's possible that, during legal maneuvering in a trial, this information would not be allowed because it could prejudice the case against the defendant, but I still need to gather as much information as I can and leave the legal matters up to the attorneys and judges.

I ask her again if Chris is using drugs. She says he uses heroin and has smoked marijuana, but nothing else. I ask her if she uses drugs. She says that five or six weeks ago she used heroin, which in my experience establishes her as a hardcore user. She says the last time she smoked marijuana was about two years ago. She says neither one of them have ever used "meth."

My game plan in this interview is to verify as much as I can about the statement Chris gave us. Reina and Chris appear to be inseparable, so to my mind both of them must know what happened to the kids. To me it's obvious that, right now, Reina would defend Chris, no matter what. Chris has already defended Reina in his statement. So, for the moment, I realize I need to treat Reina in a non-confrontational manner. This is not the moment to get tough with her. I need her cooperation. I need to gain her trust. I want to see how she reacts emotionally to my questions.

I ask her if she would ever say anything if Chris were to do something terribly wrong. She says she would tell someone. I ask her if she's ever asked him about why the kids have never been back to visit. She says she's never asked him, but thinks it's because of the situation they're in. I ask her if they've ever had the kids for a long period of time. She says they've had them off and on at different times, but no longer than a three-week period.

I ask her when was the last time she and Chris picked up the kids. She says the last time they were with the kids, they never did pick them up. She says Jamie was the one who would drop the kids off to them. I ask her when Jamie dropped them off. She says it's been a while, but she thinks it was about a year to one-and-a-half years ago.

I then confront her and tell her she's not being truthful about everything. I tell her I know they've had the kids more recently than that. She says she just doesn't know; she just works and works.

I ask her to tell me about how Chris interacted with the kids. She's evasive about answering the question. She first replies by saying she usually isn't around because, again, she just works and works. I ask her again to tell me about how Chris interacted with the kids during the time she was together with all of them. She says Chris won't talk to her about the kids or how they are. I tell her it's hard to believe that neither of them would ever talk about the kids, as close as they are to each other. She again says that all she does is just work, work, and work, and she has limited time with the family.

I then tell her I know they had the kids for months, not just weeks, as she has stated. I ask her if she knows how Chris would discipline the children. She says he would give the kids timeouts. I ask her if he ever had any problems with the kids being too active. She says he didn't, and she says he was the same with all three of the kids.

Reina again tells me about how much time she spends at work. According to her, she didn't really get a chance to see her son (little Chris) because she would have to feed and take care of all the kids when she got home. Afterwards, she would go to sleep, and then get up to go to work the next day.

I then ask her to tell me about the jobs she's had. She says she worked as a leasing agent for the Southwind Village Apartments for about six to eight months. She says she can't remember the dates or times of her employment at the Southwind Village Apartments.

I then try to work out a timeline by trying to get her to remember the jobs that she's worked, starting with January 2006. She says she was probably at the leasing office, but isn't sure. I try to use her birthday as a reference, but that doesn't help. She just says she isn't sure. There's no mention of any other jobs she held during that year. At this time, I take a break from the interview.

When I come back, I tell Reina I want to talk about the life she has with Chris. I also tell her I want to know how Chris treats her. She says he's verbally abusive, and at times he threatens to hit her, but never has. I then ask her if the kids were ever treated in the same way. She says he never treated them that way. I tell her I've spoken to his family, and they thought he was heavy-handed with them. Reina says no one is ever around the kids, so how would they know how he treats them?

I remind her that the grandparents come down every year for the rodeo. I ask her if the grandparents have ever had visitations with the kids. She says they didn't get to visit because she (Jamie) was such a "bitch" and wouldn't allow it. I then tell her I know the grandparents have spoken to the kids over the phone. She says she isn't sure about that, because she probably wasn't around. I tell her I feel she's not being honest with me, and she needs to tell the truth. She continues to be evasive with her answers.

She goes on to say that the time she spent taking care of the kids was limited because she was always working. She says that, on her days off, she sometimes would take care of them. I ask her how the kids looked when they came over for a visit. She says they were dirty and looked like they hadn't eaten. She says they were always hungry and would eat everything in the house.

I ask her if they had any problems eating. She says they had healthy appetites and never had any problems eating their food. She says they were skinny from being at Jamie's house. I then ask her if they gained any weight while they were with her and Chris. She says they might have gained some weight.

I ask her again where they were living when they last had the kids. She says they lived at the Portofino Apartments. Again, she isn't sure of the time they were living there. I ask her about the kids' sleeping arrangements. She says they mainly slept on the living room couch.

I ask her who was responsible for buying the groceries. She says she's the one who buys the food, and she spends about $300.00 per month. I ask her about her monthly income. She says she made about $700.00 every two weeks. I then ask her how much time she spent taking care of the kids. She says she didn't take care of them much because she was always working.

I ask her who Mirna is, and she says Mirna is her aunt and is like a mother to her. She says she has confided in Mirna about some of her problems. She says she did tell her about her drug use, and that she has a problem with drugs. I then ask her when was the last time she used heroin. She says she last used heroin about three months ago. She says she and Chris have used drugs together, but never in front of her son.

I ask her again when the last time they had the kids was, and when Jamie's boyfriend picked them up, but she says she doesn't know. I ask her if she misses the kids. She says she does miss them, because her son doesn't have anyone to play with. I ask if she's ever questioned Chris as to why the kids never come over for visits anymore. She says she hasn't asked because of the stress they're under.

I ask her if she's the one who cleaned their apartment. She says she's the one who cleaned it most of the time. I ask her about her routine for cleaning the apartment. Her answer is short, just that she cleaned the whole apartment. I ask her if she ever noticed any unusual smells coming from the apartment. She says she never noticed anything.

I ask her if she knows a person by the name of Joshua. She again is somewhat evasive, but does say she knows him. I ask her if she and Chris ever asked Joshua to rent a storage unit for Chris. She says no. I then ask her if she was ever with Chris and Joshua when they went to rent a storage unit. She says she never did, and there was never a need to rent storage unit, because they left all of their stuff behind when they moved.

I show her photographs of Tyler and Ariana and ask her who the kids are. She identifies them, and I then tell her they're missing. She doesn't seem to understand what I mean by missing and asks me what I mean by that. I tell her the kids are missing, and right now no one knows where they are. I tell her I want to know what Chris ever had to say to her about the kids. She says all he told her was that Jamie's boyfriend picked them up.

I ask her if she ever thought the kids might be in danger being with Jamie's boyfriend. She says she thinks they were and feels bad she never said anything to Chris about it. At this time, I feel a break is needed, and I leave the room. Reina is kept in the room and monitored.

While I'm away, I confer with Mike, and he updates me on the information he's gotten from Chris. Chris told Mike the kids are dead, and that they died while under his care. He claims that Reina doesn't know anything.

I tell Mike what Reina has said, and that I'm sure she's either holding back on what she knows or else she was a participant in the children's deaths. I decide to tell her what Chris has said about the kids to see her reaction and what she has to say about it.

I return to the room and tell Reina I have more information on the kids. I tell her the kids are dead and that Chris is the one who caused their deaths. I tell her I need to know from her what happened to the kids. She doesn't offer any new information and cries about what I've told her. She's in denial and doesn't want to believe that Chris killed the kids.

Reina never really mentions having any concern about the kids' welfare. She mainly states she doesn't believe Chris did this to the kids. Why would he ever hurt them? It seems she's more concerned for Chris than for the kids. I think she cries because she and Chris have been caught. These are not genuine tears for the kids. I truly do not feel any empathy for Reina.

At this time, I decide to take another break. I leave pictures of the kids in the room with her and tell her to look at them and think about them. I decide I'm probably not going to get any more information from her, so I decide to try another approach.

I ask Det. Lisa Lopez to go in and talk to Reina. I tell Lisa I'm hoping Reina will open up to her and be more truthful with her. Lisa has young children, and I feel that maybe the woman and mother connection will help in this. Lisa agrees and knows what

Reina has been saying because she's been watching the interview from the observation room.

Det. Lopez goes in, introduces herself to Reina, and continues the interview. However, Reina doesn't offer any new information, and the interview eventually is concluded. I tell Lisa that Reina is still holding back and knows more than she's saying. Lisa, for some reason, doesn't quite agree with me. She thinks Reina is telling the truth. I don't say too much more about it to Lisa.

Reina is released at this time. We need to verify the information she's given us before we can determine her role in the investigation.

After speaking with Reina, I go over to see how the interview is going with Chris. It seems they've taken a break or the interview has been concluded. I see through the video monitor that Chris is again becoming disorderly. He's getting on top the table and banging the cuffs on the table. He's yelling and wants some attention. I go in to calm him down and tell him he needs to settle down. As I'm leaving, he tells me the same thing he told Mike earlier. He says he wants to talk to me right now. I sit down and ask him what he wants to talk about.

He begins weeping and says it wasn't about money or child support. He says he couldn't help them, and that he "fucked up." It wasn't over money. I ask him why he kept the children if he couldn't take care of them. He says it was because he had a hard time leaving them with other people, and he didn't want to deal with that. He says he "fucked up" and made a mistake. He should have called somebody, but was too scared to call.

Chris is very erratic, jumping from one subject to the next. I'm not entirely sure what he's told Mike, but I figure it can't hurt to go back over some things, so I ask him about his drug use. He admits to using, but says it's under control. He then jumps into stating that the kids wouldn't eat, so he would feed them Cream of Wheat. He says it was "bullshit" that the kids had broken bones.

He says the kids slept in the same bed he did, and he didn't believe they were hurt because he would never do anything to hurt them. I then tell him the kids were hurt. He says he tried to make a phone call, insinuating that he wanted to get help for the kids, possibly from social services, but no one would help him because he didn't have legal custody. He says he was scared.

I remind him that he spoke to Det. Walker and ask him if he has any other information to offer. He just replies that he didn't hurt the kids. He says he was scared because we don't know what it was like to see his kids go (die) in front of him. I ask him why he was afraid. He says he was scared for his son, Christopher.

I ask him if he has any explanation for the broken ribs on Ariana. He says he didn't know anything about that, and he was never abusive to his kids. He blames his ex-wife for the domestic violence they went through and blames social services for not helping him. He says that, by the time social services got to him, something was already wrong with the kids. He says he's not a bad father, he just made some poor choices.

To me, Chris is establishing himself as a narcissistic and self-serving, manipulative person. He blames everyone else for his problems. He even blames the kids for their own deaths. He is pathetic. I do agree with him on one thing, though—that he's going to hell for this.

Ofc. Gary Parrish comes in, and I ask Gary to get Mike and tell him to come back in. Mike returns to the room, and we continue the interview. Chris says he wants to pray for his son (Chris, Jr.) and say goodbye to him. He then asks why there was only one set of bones in the "mother fucker" (tub). Mike tells him those are the only ones we know of, and that we can talk about that later.

We then advise him that we've taken a statement from Reina, who says the kids never had a problem eating and were always hungry whenever she fed them. He says Reina is sugar-coating everything. I ask him what he told Reina on the day the kids disappeared. He says he told her their mother (Jamie) picked them up. He says Reina never did ask who came over to pick up the kids.

We confront him about his father telling us that he thought Chris was heavy-handed with the kids. He says that maybe he was in the past, but he wasn't that way now. He's asked if he recently spent time with his father. He says his father was in town, and he did spend time with him while he was here.

He's then asked if his dad ever questioned him about the kids or told Chris he wanted to see them. He says he would ask all the time. He says he would lie to his dad about the kids and always tell him they were with family or friends.

Chris is asked if Reina knows what happened to the kids. He says she never knew, and he never opened up to her because they have a kid together, and he knew she would split on him. He says this was all about spending time with his son (Chris, Jr.). He's asked if this was his motive for doing what he did to Ariana and Tyler. He really doesn't have an answer.

He goes on to say that Reina was supportive of him keeping the kids. He says he couldn't let her see what was going on with the kids because they wanted to be with their mother. He says CPS wouldn't let the kids be with their mother, that they had to be with him. After he told the kids they weren't going to be with their mother, they started shutting down and not eating. He states that they were together in the tub, and they died of starvation under his care. He again states that Reina was not aware of the situation with the kids.

Other questions are asked and answered. He does not give us any more information that would lead us to the location of Tyler's body, so the interview with Chris Payne is eventually concluded. At this time, Chris Payne is booked for the murder and child abuse of Ariana Payne.

In Pima County, whenever a child is murdered there's always an additional charge of child abuse because, when the murder is committed, the act of child abuse is also committed. These are charged as a class-1 felony for the murder and class-2 felony for the child abuse.

Chris is eventually transported and booked into jail by uniformed officers. Prior to his transportation to the jail, Chris continues to talk to the uniformed officers about the kids and how they died under his care. Ofc. Brett Lemas records the spontaneous utterances and sends them to me.

Detectives Holewinski and Fuller have contacted Terry White and conducted an interview with her. It's discovered that Chris had previously listed her as an emergency contact when he was booked into the Pima County Jail. Ms. White states that she last saw Tyler and Ariana in the summer of 2006.

This is a very difficult time for us, because now we have to notify Jamie Hallam and the Barcalow family. I call Jamie and tell her we have additional information on the kids and want her and whomever she wants from her family to come down to the police station to talk about it. I tell her I'll be sending someone over to pick her up. I ask Det. Olivia Kennedy and Sgt. Tim Gilder to pick up Jamie and bring her over to the police station.

Jamie arrives with the Barcalow family. Carlos, Mike, and I are there to greet them, and we take them into one of the conference rooms. I try not to hesitate too much and just tell them the news that we strongly believe Ariana is the victim found in the storage unit, but we can't officially confirm that until the DNA results are back from the lab. I tell them the reason we strongly believe this is because it's what Chris told us during the interview.

We also tell them we're still looking for Tyler and, again, based on statements from Chris, we believe he is also dead. We tell them we'll continue to look for his body. At this time, we're not sure if he was in the storage unit and moved, or if his body was dumped in the landfill. This is difficult, and my feelings are heavy because we only recently found out about Tyler. If we had known he existed, we might have been able to find his body, so he could be buried next to his sister, Ariana.

I tell them we can't divulge much information to them at this time because this is still an on-going investigation. They seem to accept this as well as anybody could be expected to. They thank us and go on home. This was very difficult to do, but it had to be done, and the family had a right to know about the kids. I tell Jamie I will still be in contact with her and give her my office number.

I hear from other people a lot that Jamie had as much to with this as Chris and Reina. I'm not so sure. Jamie was a mother who got hooked on drugs, but the one thing she did do was take care of her kids, and whenever she couldn't she made sure that Tyler and Ariana were looked after by her family. She did protect them in this way and, when Chris never brought them back, she did look for them and tried to get them back. She did not deserve to have her kids taken away like this by their father. I would tell whoever would render this opinion how I felt about Jamie.

Jamie's stepbrother, Richard, approaches me and tells me that, as soon as he saw the news of the discovered remains of a little girl, he knew we were looking at Ariana as the possible victim. He says he put it together when Jamie told him we took buccal samples for DNA. He knew it was for identifying Ariana, and not for the custodial investigation, as we told her. I just smile at him in agreement.

The search into the Los Reales Landfill continues into the evening and is eventually stopped for the night. Uniformed officers are assigned to secure the landfill area throughout the night to preserve the scene.

After the family leaves, it's time to get back to business. We now have to prepare search warrants for the various locations, but prior to our serving of the search warrants I respond over to the Portofino Apartments and speak to the manager, Renda.

I advise her that we're requesting to serve a search warrant on apartment #2109 and ask her if she has a key to the apartment. She gives me the key and says the apartment is still vacant and has not been occupied since Chris and Reina moved out. She says they have a problem with the smell and cannot get rid of it. She also tells me that the maintenance crew went in and painted the walls. I thank her, and afterwards an officer is left at the scene to keep it secured.

Craig Arndt obtains the warrants for the following properties: Portofino Apartments, 1702 West 36th Street, Apt. #2109; Palm Court Inn, 4425 East 22nd Street, #312. These warrants include searching Chris and Reina's car at the Palm Court Inn. We decide that Carlos, Mike, and I will process the crime scene at the Portofino Apartments, #2109. Lisa, Craig, Olivia Kennedy, and Sgt. Tim Gilder will process the scene at the Palm Court Inn, #312.

TPD CSS Technicians are called and respond to photograph and assist in processing the scenes. Daniel Rushing responds to the scene at the Portofino Apartments, and Thomas Steffans goes to the Palm Court Inn. The search warrant services continue into the night and early morning hours of the next day.

Day 13: Friday, March 2, 2007

Once everyone has arrived at the Portofino Apartments #2109, we knock and announce before going in. The dispatcher is advised of the time of service and entry to officially document (protocol) the time the entire apartment was initially photographed. We then enter the apartment and see that it's full of debris and trash left behind after Chris and Reina left. We notice that the debris and trash is centered in the middle of the rooms. This is because the management ordered the apartment walls painted over in an attempt to clean up the place after Chris and Reina left. They wanted to rent it again, but that hasn't happened because of the foul odor of death.

We notice that miscellaneous paperwork and documents have been left behind. One of the documents is proof of indicia for Chris and Reina (paperwork indicating they lived there). We also notice the foul odor still lingering inside the apartment, the master bedroom closet, and the outside storage closet.

We then make our observations and begin to label the rooms and any evidence we need to collect that's asked for in the warrant. As we work our way around, I start searching the bedroom closet. I notice a square 6″ x 6″ hole near the bottom of the west wall, next to the door, which strikes me as being very odd. When I look inside, I see what appears to be dried up feces mixed with hair. I remember that, during Chris's interview, he said the kids had been eating their own feces. I'm shocked and in disbelief. It's surreal to me to imagine how much these kids must have suffered. I then tell everyone about the feces and hair; no one can believe it. These items are photographed before they're collected and placed into evidence.

When we get to the outside storage unit, I see possible dried-up body fluid/bloodstains on the wooden floor, and what appear to be possible bloodstains on the wall. I tell Carlos we need to take the floor and the section of the wall with us. We don't have the equipment to remove them, but we know the fire department does. They are called and respond. We explain what's needed and why. They take their chainsaw and cut out the entire floor and the section of the wall that we've outlined. The following items are initially collected:

#61 MPO-Section of the wooden floor from the outdoor storage room

#62 MPO-Section of drywall with bloodstains from the outdoor storage room

#63 MPO-1-pair of child shorts from the outdoor storage room

#64 MPO-1-package of checks in the name of "Reina Gonzales" located in the living room

#65 MPO-Notice of Eviction located in the living room on top of the TV

#66 MPO-Section of carpeting with red stains found in the master bedroom closet

#67-MPO-Carpet/padding/particle board with bugs &
    hair from the master bedroom closet
#68-MPO-Biological material from the inside of the
    common wall between the master bedroom and closet
    (feces & hair)
#69-MPO-Section of carpeting from the master bedroom
#70-MPO-1-small section of carpeting & padding with
    suspected bloodstain

As we're finishing up with the search warrant, we're notified by dispatch that the staff at Pima County Jail wants us to contact them because Chris Payne has told the CO's that he wants to speak to detectives about disclosing the location of Tyler's body.

At around 0245 hours, Mike and I respond to the jail to speak with Chris. The staff brings him into one of the holding rooms. When I see him, I'm hopeful that he'll finally tell us about Tyler—where he might be or what he did with him—but my hope doesn't last long.

I tell Chris it's my understanding that he wants to talk to us and tell us where Tyler's remains are. He says he does and asks us if we're ready to go for a ride. He's then reminded of his Miranda rights, but tells us he does not need an attorney.

From previous dealings with Chris, I expect he's going to try to manipulate us. I see that he wants something, and so does Mike. We look at each other, but say nothing. We decide to see how far he's willing to go with this.

I tell him we need to know what he has to say. He tells us he first wants something to eat. He then tells us that unless we get him something to eat, he's not going to help us find Tyler. He's then told that he needs to provide us with some information before we can do anything for him. He states "Tucson Mountains" (a small desert mountain range west of Tucson). We tell him he hasn't given us enough information, and we need more.

We then tell him that we'll see what we can do about getting him something to eat. I make arrangements with the Corrections Officers to see if they can get him some food. Afterward, they're able to get him a sandwich and a soda. During the wait, he tells us Tyler was in the tub with Ariana, and that he took him out of the tub. He also tells us Tyler should have been in the tub with Ariana. He then states that the "mountains" is the only other place where Tyler is.

After we deal with Chris over the food and information, he finally tells us that he buried Tyler's body in the Gates Pass/Speedway area. He tells us that Tyler is in a marked grave that only he would know. He says he gave Tyler a proper burial, and he would now be willing to take us there. I become very upset with him.

After Chris eats the sandwich and drinks his soda, he further manipulates the situation and asks for a second and, later, a third sandwich. After the second sandwich is given to him, he states that he wants an attorney, and we don't ask him any more questions. We're about to leave when Chris asks for the third sandwich. He says he'll take us to the gravesite, and then tells us he doesn't need an attorney.

We go off tape to make the arrangements to get Chris out of jail and escort him to the Gates Pass area. I call Carlos and tell him Chris is going to take us to Tyler's gravesite, and to get the picks and shovels together. As arrangements are being made to release Chris, he tells us that, if he doesn't get the third sandwich, he isn't going to take us anywhere.

Now, it's not my nature to get angry with the suspects or arrestees that I interview. My philosophy is to have the person be comfortable with you and to maintain a low-key approach. If you can gain their trust and confidence, then they will most of the time open up and talk to you.

I must say that at this point I have run out of patience, and I become angry with Chris. I yell at him and tell him we're no longer going to play his games. I tell him I can't believe he would manipulate us over his son's body just to get some food for himself. I tell him he really doesn't care for his son. I tell him we're there for his son and nothing more. I then tell Mike I've had enough of Chris, and I leave. I don't even look back to see his reaction.

Chris was booked into the jail after dinner was served and didn't get a chance to eat, so he's hungry and just playing us for that reason. As we're leaving, I tell the corrections officers that we're done with him and not to give him the third sandwich. We don't ask any him any more questions, and we never speak to Chris after that.

After Craig and Lisa search the apartment at the Palm Court Inn, they have the Plymouth Breeze towed to the main station, where it's secured in the vehicle bay. They search the car and some evidence is collected and placed into property by Craig.

This has been quite a day. We're all tired and go home. I do my best to get some sleep, but there's too much on my mind. I keep this to myself because I don't want anyone to know how much this case is stressing me emotionally and psychologically. I don't mean to insinuate that I'm becoming dysfunctional in any way, but the pressure is real, and I know I have to keep it together. I desperately want to succeed in getting justice for these kids and convicting Chris and Reina. I also know that everyone involved feels this way and, as a team, we're getting it done.

The search of Los Reales Landfill resumes and Capt. Richards requests the assistance of a recruit class at the TPD Police Academy to help. Anyone who goes out to search the landfill has to wear protective clothing. A protective body suit called a "Bunny suit," steel-toed rubber boots, surgical masks, and gloves are ordered and brought in. The command post is also sent to provide relief. The temperature is about 100-plus degrees, so we have to work in shifts and stay hydrated. TPD Air One helicopter takes photographs of the search. The search is terminated later on that day. Tyler is still missing.

We find out from the leased paperwork at the Portofino Apartments that Chris drove a 1994 Cadillac. Mike tells me he's going out to the apartments to ask the management about the car.

Once we're back at the office, we discuss whether Tyler's remains may have been in the Dumpster during the time we were initially at the scene. We're not sure if Diane was telling us the truth or if she left out some information. We're thinking that maybe she dumped Tyler's body before she called the police, and that it was later picked up by the dump truck. Another theory discussed is whether either Chris or Reina went back and picked up Tyler's body, disposed of it somewhere else, and left Ariana's in the storage locker.

When I initially hear that Tyler was possibly in the tub with Ariana, my heart sinks. I'm stunned. It never occurred to me that there might be a second body in the Dumpster. At the time, there was nothing to suggest that there might have been another body inside. Now I'm second-guessing myself and asking myself why I didn't empty out all the contents of the Dumpster. I certainly considered it, but I thought to myself at the time that the evidence presented was the tub, lid, canvas bag, and plastic garbage bag. I did look inside the Dumpster and did not see anything that would indicate another body in the Dumpster.

I find out later that Diane said she saw a Dumpster diver inside the Dumpster later that evening, after we had left the scene. This means it's possible the diver might have disturbed the scene. Tyler's body could have been moved towards the lower part of the Dumpster. When the other tenants filled the Dumpster, their trash covered him up. I'm not sure what to think, and I still second-guess myself. It's difficult to deal with, but I know that Mike and I still have work to do. We press on.

Capt. Richards tells me it's not my fault that the Dumpster wasn't searched. He says he was a homicide detective at one time, and even he didn't think of emptying the contents of the Dumpster. My colleagues are also very supportive and reassure me that no one knew Tyler was a second victim, and it isn't my fault. This helps, but for the longest time I'm guilt-ridden for not finding Tyler's body.

When I speak to Prosecuting Attorney Sue Easer about it, she's sure that Tyler's body was in the Dumpster, but wants to do another interview with Diane just to see what she has to say about it. Sue tells me the reason she believes Tyler was still in the tub is because of the pour marks that were inside the tub.

Carlos informs me that he did contact Diane Hanselman again to insure that nothing other than the Rubbermaid tub had been in locker #C19 and to confirm what she had seen and described in the tub. This interview is audio-recorded and a copy of the CD is given to me.

Mike and I press on and decide to try and find Reina again. We know she still has a lot to offer in the investigation, and we believe she's involved in the kids' deaths. We need to conduct another interview with her. As we're driving around trying to find her, I receive a call from one of her aunts, who tells me Reina has checked into Compass Healthcare for drug rehabilitation. She also tells me she's willing to call me and give me any information whenever she talks to Reina, but she wants to remain anonymous. She says Reina is close to her and will probably give her information about the kids and what happened to them.

We respond to the health care facility. After speaking with the staff, we're told we're not allowed to speak with Reina. At first, they won't even acknowledge she's there. Then they do go back and ask her if she wants to talk to us. Of course, she doesn't.

I call Cassie Dixon, the CPS caseworker, and leave her a message to call me back. When she calls back, I ask her when her next visitation is with Reina and little Chris. She tells me her next visitation is set for Monday, 03-05-07 at 8:00 a.m.

After this, Sgt. Valdez calls and states that he's received a phone call from Mr. B's Rental. They told him they have a couch with two missing cushions that was returned to them in January/07, and Reina and Chris had rented the couch. We respond to the business, but upon examining the couch nothing of evidentiary value is seen or found.

While Mike and I are driving around, I turn to him and tell him I appreciate his help. I tell him that, of all the detectives, I'm glad he's the one working with me on this case. I tell him that everyone works differently and at his or her own pace. Our unit works out the call out rotation on a weekly basis. You are eventually paired up with each detective in the unit and get to know how they work. I tell him that, when you're paired up with another detective, you realize you work better with some detectives than with others. I feel that Mike and I work at the same pace, think alike, and move along in our investigations. I tell Mike that this is one case where we had to move quickly and stay aggressive. Mike and I have always worked well together. This is not to demean anyone in our unit; I've worked with them all, and I've never had a problem working with anyone. But I've always moved quickly and aggressively in my investigations, and Mike is the same way. I know that, at times, I become too headstrong, and I know I need to slow it down, but sometimes it's hard. My supervisors have also advised me of this.

Day 16: Monday, March 5, 2007

Detectives Holewinski and Fuller are assigned to try and locate Chris Navarro. Mr. Navarro is listed as having been the manager who rented storage locker #C19 to Joshua Neuser. They find him and advise me that he's not very cooperative and doesn't want to be involved.

Detectives Holewinski and Musgrave are assigned to speak with the manager at the Portofino Apartments again and get additional information on Chris and Reina from their neighbors. When they come back, they tell me the management spoke with Reina in early

August 2006 at her apartment. They told her the rent was past due, and they were starting the eviction process. Chris overheard this and began yelling at Reina from inside the apartment. The management then decided to leave because they felt that Chris was a violent person, and they didn't want to be around while this was going on.

Afterwards, the two detectives go over to Apt. #2110 and speak with Ronald Genung. During the interview, he states that he did meet Chris and Reina. At first, they were friendly, but after he filed a complaint to the management about loud music coming from their apartment, they were not too friendly. He does say that, since last July/August 2006, there was a smell of what he thought was a dead animal coming from their apartment.

It's about 7:45 a.m. when Mike and I respond to the CPS office at 6363 South Country Club to meet with Reina. Reina is there with other family members for her visit with Chris Jr. We let her finish her visit and afterwards ask her for another interview. I tell her that, based on information we've received, we have more questions to ask. She agrees to be re-interviewed, and her family brings her over to the main station. She's taken to the interrogation room, and the interview is again recorded on video.

She is again read her Miranda rights. She tells us she understands them and is willing to answer our questions. She's asked about the drug use. She tells us that Chris is a heroin dealer and uses his own product. She tells us she also used heroin, and they preferred to smoke it instead of using the needle. She says recently she's gone into rehabilitation, and the last time she used was about a month ago.

We go over the history between her, Chris, and the children. She says she and Chris met in 2002 and describes their relationship as rocky, at first. She's asked about how visitations were set up with Tyler and Ariana. At first, she says Chris initially had visitations a couple of times, and then she says four or five times. She's asked how often they moved. She tells us they've moved about three times within the last six months.

Reina is asked if she was aware of the child support payments that Chris had to pay. She says she didn't know about them, and that the money she earned was going out to pay for food and rent. She says she would even buy the kids whatever they needed because she treated them as if they were her own children.

She says that every time Jamie would bring them to the house, they were always dirty, hungry, skinny, and smelly. She says she got to know Tyler and Ariana when they lived with them at the Portofino Apartments. She's asked if the kids gained any weight during the time they were living with her and Chris. She says she thinks they might have gained a little bit.

She says she was working full time, forty hours or more a week, and that the kids were properly taken care of by Chris. She says she didn't see him mistreat any of the kids. She says that, when she came home, she did spend time with the kids, mostly in the evening.

She says that, after about two months, Jamie and her boyfriend came over and picked up the kids. She says she thought they were still with Jamie or Jamie's family after that. She does say the kids were probably picked up before October, or maybe sometime when the lease was up, but she's not sure. She says she has a problem remembering dates and times.

She says she and Chris did apply for food stamps and assistance, and that they listed Tyler and Ariana. She says Chris, Jr. was the main child they used when they applied for assistance. She says she doesn't know why they listed Tyler and Ariana, but knew they did need the assistance. She says that, whenever the kids wanted to speak to Jamie, Chris would call her, but she never answered.

Reina says the kids didn't want to live with Jamie because she would always leave them with strangers. She says Tyler was mainly the one who would tell her about that. She told Tyler that, if his dad wanted them to stay, then they could. Reina says she would feed the kids and take time away from her son to take care of them.

We then question Reina about Tyler and Ariana's physical development. She describes them as being normal, with Ariana having some pee accidents every now and then. She's asked if Chris ever took the children on outings for fun. She says he really didn't do that.

She's asked if the kids ever misbehaved. She says they usually didn't, that they were calm and liked to watch TV. She says there was never any indication of anything happening while she was at work. She's asked if she ever saw any injuries on the kids. She says they never complained about getting hurt at all.

She's asked if the kids were okay on the day Jamie picked them up. She says they were fine when she left for work, and they slept in that morning. She says that was the last time she saw the kids. She says they ate really well, watched TV, and were happy the day before they left.

She does say she thought it was strange when Jamie and her boyfriend suddenly showed up to pick them up. She thought this was strange because Chris could never get in touch with Jamie before then. She says she never did question Chris about the kids being picked up and or why they left.

She's asked if she ever went into the bedroom closet to get toys for Chris, Jr. She says she didn't go in there very often because most of his toys were usually out, but occasionally she did go in. She says that, most of the time, the kids would go in and get their own toys.

I ask her if she's aware that, ever since they moved out of their Portofino apartment, it has never been rented. She says she wasn't aware of that. She's asked about their sleeping arrangements at the Portofino apartment. She says the kids slept in the bedroom, and she, Chris, Jr., and Chris would sleep in the living room.

She's asked about the outdoor storage closet and if she knew what was kept inside. She says she never went inside, but thought there might be a bike stored there. She says she would sleep near the closet (contradiction) and walked by it every day because it was by the front door. We then tell her that there's evidence indicating Tyler was kept in the bedroom closet. She becomes very defensive and says she wasn't aware of anything.

She says she went to visit Chris at the jail because she wanted to know why he had done this to the kids. She says that, during the visit, he told her it wasn't as bad as she thought, but apologized to her and asked her forgiveness for what he had done. I ask her why he asked for forgiveness. She says she can't remember what he said. She says she just assumed he was apologizing for killing his kids because she'd heard it on the news. She says she doesn't know what to believe. She says it was very emotional when she spoke to him at the jail.

We tell her that Chris told us she never lived with him at the Portofino Apartments. She says she doesn't know why he would say that, because she was on the lease. She's asked if she ever noticed the bad smell that was in the apartment. She says she didn't notice the smell. I tell her we were in the apartment as of last week, and the smell is still there. She's told it would be impossible for her not to have known.

She still denies smelling the foul odor. She says that, if she had smelled it or had known anything, she would have done something to help the kids. She wouldn't have just let it go, because she considered them to be like her own.

She's asked about the holes in the wall inside her apartment. She says she only remembers one hole in the apartment, and that was in the bedroom. She says Chris punched the wall because he was angry. We tell her about the other holes inside the apartment.

We press her again about the smell inside the apartment. She still says she never noticed it. She's told that after six months we still notice the smell. She's told that she knows more than she's telling us. She denies this and says if she knew more she would tell us. We then confront her with some of her inconsistencies. We remind her that, during her first interview, she told us they only had the kids for three weeks, when at that time we knew they'd had them for two months.

We tell her we know about the custody issues between Chris and Jamie. We tell her we now know she and Chris had the kids for at least six months. She's reminded that she told us there was no domestic violence between them, and now she's telling us there was. She keeps denying that she's lied about anything.

We ask how she took care of the kids. She goes into detail about how good she was with them and Chris Jr. We confront her and tell her it seems to us as if she cared more for Chris, Jr. than for Tyler and Ariana. She's asked again if she ever saw any injuries on the kids. She says she never saw the kids being hurt or injured. She says they were perfectly fine. I then tell her that Ariana had suffered some broken bones, and she had to know about that. She tells us she never knew, and Ariana never told her anything about getting hurt.

She's asked about the property they left behind at the apartment on Stone. She says they left most of their property behind because they were evicted. They decided to just take their clothes over to their new apartment at the Palm Court Inn.

She's asked if Chris's grandparents ever asked her about the kids. She says they never did ask her, but they might have asked Chris about them. We tell her that the grandparents told us she was around when they asked Chris about them. She says they never asked her about them, but she did think that they were with Jamie. She says she never spoke to Chris about his parents asking him about the kids and didn't know what they ever spoke about.

She's then asked if she would be willing to take a polygraph test. She says she's telling us the truth and doesn't want to take the test at this time. She says she wants to think about it, but feels she doesn't need to take it. (She never does take the test.)

We stop talking to her and again bring Lisa in to continue interviewing her. Lisa is being extremely low key with her and goes over the same basic questions. Reina does not disclose anything new.

Police Chief Richard Miranda is aware of the investigation and Chris's arrest. A press conference is set up and conducted at the Main Police Station. He speaks at the conference and states that we've made an arrest. He briefly speaks about the children and says this is still an on-going investigation. I sit in the back row, listening, and see that most of the media in the Tucson area are there.

Day 17: Tuesday, March 6, 2007

Dr. Anderson from OME calls me and tells me he has more information on Ariana. Mike and I go over to the OME office and meet with him. He advises us that he's discovered additional injuries on Ariana. He says she sustained a broken spine that could be peri-mortum (at or near the time of death) or that could have been inflicted after she died and occurred after she was placed in the tub. He can't give me a timeline of the injury.

You should know that there are three stages of time in which an injury can occur. One is premonitory, which means before the person passed away or pre-warning; peri-mortum, which means the injury could have happened at or near the time of death, even, in some bones, up to two weeks after the death (the tissue is still functioning and could still show signs of healing. However, this will only last for a short period of time, and that didn't happen in this case); and postmortem, which is after death.

Dr. Anderson says Ariana suffered a broken shoulder from an impact, and he has discovered an additional broken rib. He takes out the related bones and shows us the injuries. I call for a TPD Crime Scene Technician to respond. When he has, I have him take pictures of the additional fractured bones.

After that, we go back to the office. Mike decides to conduct a title search on the 1994 Cadillac. The information is received from MVD. Sean and Lisa go over to the Portofino Apartments to get additional information about the neighbors and the tow truck company.

While they're doing this, I receive a call from Carolina Calderon, who tells me she's a friend of Reina's, and she has information on the kids and wants to talk about it. I don't let her off the phone and quickly set up my recorder. I tell her what I'm doing and conduct the telephonic interview. I ask her general questions and, after she's answered them, I move toward asking her about the information she wants to disclose.

She tells me she last saw the children at the Portofino Apartments from late July to mid-August 2006. She states that, during that time, she saw Tyler with a bruise on his face and quietly asked him about it. Tyler told her Chris had hit him. She comforted him and told him she would try to get some help for him. She then states that, after the visit, she called the Child Abuse Hotline and left an anonymous tip.

We conduct research into the Child Abuse Hotline and discover there are no records of the call she says she made. I call her back and tell her there's no record of the call. She states that, when she made the call, she just gave the address and not an apartment number, so they never knew where to go in the complex. She then tells me this was the last time she saw the children.

Detectives Holewinski and Lopez find out that the Midnight Towing Company had the towing contract for Portofino Apartments. When the towing company is called, the staff informs them there's no record of a Cadillac being towed from the complex.

I speak with Nora Rankin and ask her what's required for additional DNA testing and analysis. She informs me that another set of buccal swabs will be needed from Jamie Hallam and Reina Gonzales in order to develop a DNA profile to compare with the evidence that's been collected.

I contact Jamie and advise her that we need another set of swabs for DNA analysis and further testing. Mike and I meet with her and take the buccal samples that are needed. We speak cordially to her and ask her how she's doing. She looks to me like she's in a state of depression. I can tell she's probably using "meth." She says CPS is on her case with the baby she recently had and are conducting another investigation on her. She says she's not doing very well.

Mike and I tell her she needs to get herself together for her baby daughter, or she'll lose her, too. We tell her that, somehow, she needs to kick the habit and get her life back on track. We tell her we're concerned for her welfare. She knows this and says she's trying.

Later, I place the new buccal samples into property as evidence. It should be noted that on March 1, 2007, a set of buccal swabs was obtained from Chris Payne as part of the original search warrant. Chris and Jamie's set of swabs are listed as items:

#20MPO 1-set of buccal swabs from Chris Payne
#21MPO 4-buccal swabs from Jamie Hallam

Day 18: Wednesday, March 7, 2007

Mike and I meet with Deputy Pima County Attorneys Sue Eazer and Bunkye Chi at the Portofino Apartments #2109. They want to review the scene for themselves and go over it. The apartment has been locked down, so I obtain the key from the management. The trash and other items are still there. We explain the crime scene and go over most of the areas where the collected items were found. During the course of doing this, we collect other items that may be possible evidence. These are placed into property as evidence. They are listed as items:

#71MPO-Envelope containing documents 1-letter, 1-pay
    stub, 1-business card with phone number
#73MPO-Envelope containing documents 3-photographic
    negatives
#74MPO-Envelope containing black metal container with
    residue and drug paraphernalia

During the course of the investigation, I've obtained information from the detective monitoring the 88-Crime tip line. Lisa and Craig are assigned to re-interview auctioneer Laurie Jones and Diane Hanselman regarding an 88-Crime tip on the location of Tyler's body. Craig also interviews Rusty Jones (auctioneer). They also decide to check locker #C19 again at the U-Store-It business. They see some strange pattern marks next to the outline of the tub. They note this and tell me about it.

Research into the Cadillac reveals that it was towed away from the Portofino Apartments at the request of the management. Detective Fuller is assigned to speak with Brian Bluder, Desert Towing at Ft. Lowell/Oracle. He then conducts a recorded interview with Mr. Bluder, who provides the history on the Cadillac.

On 10/26/06 the Cadillac was towed to the Desert Towing lot at East Ft Lowell. The vehicle had front end damage and two flat tires. They noted nothing unusual. They did not look in the trunk. Brian Bluder says he received a call from Forrest Payne, asking about the storage fees and what it would cost to get the car back. Mr. Bluder told him the fees were $500-$600. Mr. Payne said he had bought the car for his son, but didn't know where he was. He said he didn't have the money to get the car out of storage and would send Mr. Bluder the title. After Bluder received the title, he towed the car to DriveTime Auto and used it as a trade-in on another car. DriveTime fixed up the Cadillac and sold it to Brenda Ramirez on 03/09/06.

Mike, Carlos, and I discuss Reina's involvement in the case. We're all in agreement that she's involved and, based on all the lying she's done so far, it's obvious she knows more than she's told us. We decide to bring her back in for a third interview. I call Cassie Dixon and ask her if she might know where we can find Reina. She tells me Reina has a scheduled meeting in the morning.

Day 19: Thursday, March 8, 2007

Mike and I respond to the CPS Office and find Reina. She's asked to come down to the police station to conduct another interview. Cassie provides her with a ride to the main station. I ask a female detective to go in with me to interview her again. I ask Calvin to monitor and set up the video system. During the time we're getting ready, Sue is contacted and decides to come down with Bunkye to observe the interview.

As I'm preparing to begin the interview, I ask Cal if he knows where the detective is. At first, he doesn't know, but tells me he's going to set up the video system. I'm looking for the detective who is assisting prior to beginning the interview, and I can't find her. Cal comes back and tells me she's already interviewing Reina. I'm now upset and can't believe this. Cal has started the video, and I'm watching the detective with Reina. I then ask Cal if the detective has covered the Miranda rights with Reina. He says he doesn't think so. I then tell him to get her out of there.

Whenever a person is brought into the police station, you need to consider whether that person feels as if they're being detained. In this case, Reina is a suspect and, even though she did volunteer to come down again, she has been placed in a detention room to be interviewed. I know she needs to have her Miranda rights read to her again. We're going to ask her incriminating questions, and she's being detained, which are the two requirements set forth by the U.S. Supreme Court.

The detective comes out, and we disagree over what she's done. She expresses to us that she really feels Reina doesn't know anything about what happened to the kids. I tell her she's wrong and feel that, if Sue agrees with me, then we need to arrest Reina if she doesn't disclose anything new.

I ask the detective if she covered the Miranda rights with Reina. Her face turns red, and I know by the look in her eyes that she didn't. I tell her to go back in and finish the interview, but to cover the Miranda rights. Fortunately, she hasn't proceeded too far with the interview, and only general questions were asked before she came out. We're all watching the interview from here on, and Reina basically gives the same story and information.

Sue tells me she's seen enough, and we're ready to arrest Reina. I then interrupt the interview and ask the detective if Reina has come up with any new information. She tells me no. I then tell Reina that she's under arrest for child abuse. Reina is shocked. She's handcuffed and remains there until uniformed officers arrive to transport her to Pima County Jail.

When we get outside the interview room, the detective explodes and yells that Reina had nothing to do with this, and we're wrong. She tells me we shouldn't be making any arrests just because Sue tells us to. I'm sure Sue heard the detective say this before she left. I pull her into one of the meeting rooms. Carlos and Lt. Hovden are there. I explain to her why she's wrong.

I tell her that Reina knows exactly what happened to those kids. I tell her Chris and Reina are inseparable; they do their drugs together, they will tell each other about what is going on, and they will cover for one another. I tell her that Ariana and Tyler were an inconvenience to them and were unwanted by Reina because of the connection to Jamie. I tell her I believe that Reina wanted herself and little Chris to be Chris's only family.

I also tell her that Reina has been lying from the beginning. She lied about how long they had the kids. She lied about not noticing the smell of death in the apartment. She lied about knowing that Ariana was in pain from the injuries she had. She lied about working all the time when, in fact, there was no record of her working since the beginning of 2007.

She's been evasive all along about dates and times, saying she can't remember. She knows Chris lied to the family about the kids' whereabouts whenever they asked about them. She's even told the family the same lies whenever she was asked about their whereabouts.

Somehow, Reina apparently sucked this detective into believing her story. She's a very good detective, and I've never encountered anything like this before. I was surprised and had not expected this from her. She later tells Mike and I that we're wrong about Reina, and we'll be sorry when this goes to trial and the truth comes out about her. Mike and I look at each other and just stay quiet about her comment. I'm thinking that her judgment is temporarily skewed, and she is just making a bad assessment in this case.

Reina is transported to Pima County Jail by uniformed officers and booked. I meet with Deputy County Attorney Bunkye Chi at her office, and the case on Chris Payne is issued.

Day 20: Friday, March 9, 2007

Detectives Lopez and Walker, Captain Richards, Lt. Hovden, and I respond to the U-Store-It, #C19 to re-examine the interior. Lisa points out the pattern marks where the tub had been placed. TPD Crime Scene Technicians are called. Photographs are taken of the pattern marks, and swabs are taken. We decide to spray Luminol in the storage unit. There's evidence of blood in two small areas. These are photographed and swabs are taken. These are listed as items:

#JJ1-2-swabs of possible DNA from the south end of the floor
#JJ2-2-swabs of possible DNA from the north end of the floor
#JJ3-2-swabs of possible DNA from the south wall
#JJ4-2-swabs of possible DNA from the south floor of the unit
#JJ5-2-swabs of possible DNA from the north floor of the unit

Since small traces of blood were found at the storage unit, I decide to Luminol apartment #2109 at the Portofino Apartments. We speak with the crime scene technicians, and they say the best time to Luminol the apartment would be at night. Arrangements are made with the management, and their consent is given. They provide me with the key to the apartment. I'm told the apartment was recently painted.

Upon arrival, I meet with CSS Jennifer Sanchez #49175 and William Greener #29135. I advise them that the apartment has recently been painted and ask them if this will be a problem. They tell me that, as long as the paint is a water-based paint, then the Luminol should still work.

They process the scene, and Luminol is sprayed in the master bedroom closet, the storage room, and on the bedroom rug. The Luminol takes effect, and traces of blood are seen mainly in the master bedroom closet. As the scene is processed and labeled, they are photographed, collected, and placed into property as evidence. The following is a list of the collected items:

#3-4BG-1-item of carpeting with 2-areas of blood
#5BG-1-section of drywall with bloodstains from
    bedroom closet
#6BG-1-section of drywall with bloodstains from
    bedroom closet
#7BG-1-section of padding from bedroom closet with
    bloodstains

Mike and I go out and examine the Cadillac that was towed away from Portofino Apartments and later purchased by Brenda Ramirez. We do not find any evidence.

Day 23: Monday, March 12, 2007

I present the case on Chris to the Grand Jury. I later find out that he's indicted on 1st degree murder and child abuse.

I call Mr. Gary Gorbakovsky, the owner of the apartments at North Stone, and ask him about Chris Payne and Reina Gonzales. He remembers them and confirms that they left most of their property behind when they left. He sent a notification letter to them advising them that, if they were not picking up their items, the apartment owner would dispose of their property.

He says that, when no reply was received, their property was thrown away or sold. He says that, before they disposed of it, they took photographs of the property and made an inventory list. I ask him if he would be willing to get me a copy of the inventory list and photographs. He says he'll get them for me. Det. Fuller is advised of the list and photographs. He later meets with Mr. Gorbakovsky and picks up the list and CD. This is placed into property as evidence.

Day 26: Thursday March 15, 2007

I meet with Pima County Attorney Bunkye Chi and issue the case on Reina Gonzales for child abuse. I go back to the office and play catch up on a backlog of paperwork.

Day 30: Monday March 19, 2007

I present the case on Reina Gonzales to the Grand Jury. I later find out that she's indicted on child abuse charges.

Day 39: Wednesday March 28, 2007

I receive a call from the staff at the jail to tell me that inmate Maria A. Perez, who used to babysit for Chris and Reina, wants to talk to the police. Sean and I respond to the Pima County Jail and conduct an interview with Maria. The interview is videotaped.

Maria states that on several occasions when Chris and Reina lived at the apartments on North Stone, she used to babysit little Chris in exchange for heroin. She says she never saw or knew of Tyler and Ariana. She really does not have any other information to offer.

Days 40-41: Thursday-Friday, March 29-30, 2007

Sue Eazer informs us that she would like to re-interview Diane Hanselman. Ms. Hanselman has moved recently to Boulder City,

Nevada. Sue, Sean, and I travel to Boulder City and meet with Ms. Hanselman. Sue and I conduct a recorded interview with her.

Diane gives us a little more detail on the discovery of Ariana inside the tub. At times, she becomes upset and emotional during the interview. She has a difficult time believing she almost didn't report this to the police and nearly threw away Ariana's body without knowing it was there.

She again goes over the sequence of events of the incident. She's asked to go over the details about the tub itself. She draws a diagram showing how the lid was positioned on the tub as she was lifting it into the Dumpster. She also says the Tommy Hilfiger bag was near the top of the tub, and that it seemed to weigh about 40-50 pounds. She says she's able to estimate the weight because she has a niece who probably weighs forty pounds. She uses a facsimile prop she has at the house to demonstrate the position of the lid during the time she was lifting the tub into the Dumpster.

She also says she saw that the canvas bag was near the top of the tub after the lid had popped off a little bit. The body fluid was also at least an inch to two inches deep, and some of it did seep into the storage room floor. This means that so much body fluid built up in the tub as the body or bodies decayed that it seeped through the plastic of the tub.

All of the other information she gives us is consistent with her previous statements. After the interview, we catch a plane back to Tucson.

The interview with Diane in Boulder City is consistent with Sue's theory that Tyler's body was in the Dumpster, but I'm still not totally convinced, even though it makes sense. If the kids had been starved, then it's possible they both could have fit inside the tub.

What's confusing is the fact that Chris said he placed Tyler in the tub first, and then Ariana. Tyler was wrapped up in a black plastic bag. When Diane dumped the tub, she didn't hear or see anything roll out of it. It would also seem that, if Ariana were in the tub on top of Tyler, then she would have been the one to fall out of the tub, and not Tyler. This is why, at the time, we disagreed with Sue, but understood we needed to continue and go ahead with what information we had.

I now believe Tyler was in the Dumpster, and his body went to the landfill. Again, this will stay with me for the rest of my life. More than anything, I wanted to find his body, so he could be buried next to Ariana, bringing some closure to Jamie and the families, too.

Day 46: Wednesday, April 4, 2007

We decide to continue to look for Tyler's remains in the Gates Pass area. We spend almost the entire morning out there, digging in potential spots. What we look for are areas where it appears that the dirt has been disturbed and has somewhat of a rise to it. The search is concluded and the remains of Tyler's body haven't been found.

Chief Miranda and some of his staff are aware of what we're doing and drive over. They arrive as we're just about done. They make fun of us because of how we're dressed. It's hot, and we're wearing our worst clothes and hats to protect ourselves from the heat. We're very dirty at that point. The Chief knows that what we're doing is important and just comes over to show his support.

Day 47: Thursday, April 5, 2007

The staff from the jail advises us that another inmate, Kathleen Scott, believes Tyler was sold to drug dealers because Chris owed them money. Lisa and I have cleared the air with each other. She's still an important part of the investigation. I ask her to respond with me over to Pima County Jail and conduct the videotaped interview with Kathleen. Kathleen states she believes Tyler was sold to drug dealers because Chris owed a lot of money to his heroin connection.

She says she doesn't have any evidence or proof, and that it's purely speculation on her part that Tyler was sold to a drug dealer. Other questions are asked and answered, and the interview is concluded.

Day 49: Saturday, April 7, 2007

A second search into the Los Reales landfill is decided upon in an attempt to find Tyler's body. Cadaver dogs are used, but are not that effective because of all the contamination of rotting meat, dead animals, and various odors. Some bones are located, and Dr. Bruce Anderson from OME is called. He responds and, after examining the bones, he decides to take custody of them.

Carlos calls me and advises that Det. John Dorer has received a call from the staff at the Pima County Jail advising that inmate Hortencia Barcelo has information she wants to share about the Payne case. I'm advised that Ms. Barcelo wants to speak to the detectives about it, and that the information is about Tyler.

Carlos and I respond to the jail and conduct the interview with Ms. Barcelo. The interview is videotaped. After she answers some general questions, we ask her about the information she's received. Ms. Barcelo states that she was moved into the same cell with Reina Gonzales and Amber Olague last Thursday. She says that, soon after she was moved in with them, Reina started talking to her about the case.

Reina told her that she and Chris were under the influence of heroin, and that they had cut Tyler up into three pieces. They wrapped him up in clear plastic cellophane wrap and placed him in the tub with Ariana. Afterward, the tub was put into the storage room. She said that, after a couple of hours, they decided to take Tyler out to the landfill and place him in a small freezer, where the appliances are stored.

She says she doesn't know the name of the landfill, but does describe the Los Reales Landfill. She's then asked if she has been listening to the news on the case. She says she's heard some of it, but not that much, because the TV at the jail is broken. She also states that she's read the file Reina keeps with her from her attorney. This means that, because she's read Reina's file, her statement is tainted. She could come up with any story to try and cut a deal with the attorneys.

Carlos and I also receive information from the staff at the landfill that Huron Valley Steel Corporation is contracted to pick up appliances from the landfill. They're then placed on a conveyor belt, shredded into small pieces, and the metal is recycled. This information is passed on to the Pima County Attorney's Office. To me, this is another possible lead that needs to be looked at. Later on, Mike and I meet with the manager of the plant and discuss the protocols. We're also given a tour of the plant and shown how everything works.

It should be noted that numerous leads come in and are investigated. None of them are found to be useful or factual.

Day 51: Monday, April 9, 2007

At this time, I need to check on the validity of Hortencia Barcelo's statement. Mike and I respond to the jail and conduct an interview with Amber Olague, the other cellmate of Reina and Hortencia. The interview is videotaped at the jail.

She confirms that Ms. Barcelo was placed into the same cell with her and Reina. She states that she saw Ms. Barcelo go through Reina's court file and suspects she also went through hers. She states that Reina and Hortencia did speak with each other, but mainly in Spanish.

She says she was there, but tried not to get involved. She says she just wants to keep to herself and tries not to pick up on others' conversations. Amber is not that cooperative, and the interview is concluded. The statement that Ms. Hortencia gave does not prove to be valid or useful.

Day 52: Tuesday, April 10, 2007

Mike and I respond to HVS West (Huron Valley Steel Corporation) at 6581 East Drexel and conduct a recorded interview with Scott Laughlin, the plant manager. He states that the company is under contract to recycle and salvage the appliances at Los Reales Landfill.

He states that, after they receive the appliances, they are crushed, shredded, and all that's left is the metal itself. He states that the person who picks up the appliances doesn't really check for what might be inside. He says the freezer would have been shredded by now with nothing left. He then gives us a tour of the plant and its operation. After other questions are asked and answered, the interview is concluded.

We decide to conduct another search into the Gates Pass area for Tyler's remains. This time, cadaver dogs are brought in, and there is a "hit" on an area. This area is marked and flagged. It's late in the afternoon, so the search is continued the next day.

Day 53: Wednesday, April 11, 2007

Other detectives and I search the Gates Pass area that has been marked and flagged. After digging into the marked area, pieces of a bag with some bones and possible fur are found. These are collected, and I take them over to OME office and meet with Dr. Anderson. He states that the bones and fur are from a cat. He also tells me that the bones he collected at the Los Reales Landfill are the remains of an animal.

Another tip has come in that a smell and possible remains have been located in an area on the east side of Tucson. Sean and I drive to the remote area and search it. Tyler's remains are not found. We come back to the office.

I receive another 88-Crime tip that an associate of Chris and Reina has disclosed some information to the caller. The person with the information wants to remain anonymous and leaves a phone number. When I call the number, the person who answers the phone tells me that the information they received is coming from a friend. The anonymous caller says they told the friend to talk to me, the friend agreed, and I am given the friend's phone number. I make the call and record the interview. He says he did speak to Reina about Tyler. He says Reina told him that Chris told her that Tyler was wrapped in a plastic bag separate from Ariana and placed next to the tub inside the storage unit.

He says he spoke to Reina about two weeks ago. He says he's known them about four or five years. He says he also knew all three kids. He says that the last time he saw the kids was around last October or November, but he isn't really sure. He says that was the last time he saw all of the kids. After that, the only child he saw with them was little Chris. He says that, when he saw the kids, they looked skinny, but seemed to be okay. He says that, when Chris and Reina were at the Palm Court Inn, the kids were not with them.

He says Reina told him she never knew what Chris did to the kids. She said the kids were together, and that Tyler was in a bag, and someone had separated them. He says she told him they were both in the storage unit. He says Reina has spoken to him at least twice since all of this took place. She also told him she couldn't believe Chris would do something like this.

He goes on to tell me what he knows of the history between Chris, Jamie, and Reina. He says he knew Reina and Chris were having problems. Whenever he and Chris were together, Chris would tell him that he missed his kids. He never asked Chris where they were, but thought they were with Jamie. He says he could probably get more information from Chris and would be willing to call me with the information.

Day 65: Monday, April 23, 2007

The OME autopsy report on the possible remains of Ariana is finalized and sent over to me. I know that the media will be asking for the autopsy report. I ask Dr. Peters not to release it to them because this is still an on-going investigation, and I want to clear it first through the Pima County Attorney's Office. He says he'll tell the media that, so they won't continue to ask for it. Eventually, the report will be released to them.

The rest of the day, I stay in the office to catch up on administrative work (reports, calls, and paperwork).

Day 68: Thursday, April 26, 2007

Robin Johnson is the friend that Diane Hanselman called and asked about what to do with the Rubbermaid tub with the awful smell. I call Ms. Johnson in Texas and conduct a telephonic interview with her.

I ask her about the phone call she received from Diane back in February 2007. She tells me Diane was never one to call first because of the free long distance service that she (Robin) receives on her phone. Ms. Johnson says they spoke about the smelly tub and the "goo" inside of it. Diane told her she thought it was an animal. Robin told Diane she didn't think it was and told her she needed to call the police, just to make sure.

Diane apparently did that because Robin says she later received e-mail from Diane telling her that she was right. She called Diane and was told that a child was found in the tub. Diane told her she was having a hard time dealing with what was found. Robin confirms that she's an EMT. She also answers other questions, and the interview is concluded.

Edward Lopez was the downstairs neighbor when Chris and Reina were living at the Portofino Apartments. I call and ask to meet with him to conduct an interview about Chris, Reina, and the children. A time is arranged, and I go over to his work and conduct the interview.

Mr. Lopez confirms that he was the neighbor who lived downstairs from Chris and Reina. He says he didn't have much interaction with them, but does recall Reina coming over once to use the phone. He says that, at the time, he didn't even know their names.

He says he remembers banging noises coming from their apartment, and how loud they were. He says it sounded like they were moving stuff or dropping things at night. He says he only saw one child and thinks he was about one or two years old. He says that, most of the time, he would hear Reina yelling at the child for spilling something or for not going to sleep. He says he did complain to the management about the excessive noise. He says the disturbances would occur about three times a week.

He says he thought they had a Cadillac that was broken down. He says he doesn't recall a bad smell ever coming from the apartment. Mr. Lopez says he knew they had left because the noise stopped. He says he does remember that the car was left behind. He remembers that Chris came back to the apartment after they left. He goes on to answer additional questions, and then the interview is concluded.

Day 69: Friday, April 27, 2007

I call Professor Carl Olsen and ask to meet with him to do an interview and to speak about the insects I left with him. Mike and I go over to his office and record the interview. I've also brought additional insects that I collected at the scene of the Portofino Apartments, #2109, and ask him to give me an opinion on those insects. He looks at all of them and describes what they are. He says that the pupa is a flesh-eating insect that has gone through a metamorphosis.

He goes into the forensics of the insects and explains how they collected inside the tub. He describes how they move, evolve, and survive in a decomposing body. He says the insects I brought are all of the same species. After interviewing him, we thank him and leave.

I receive a call from "Carrie," who is related to Chris. She tells me that a friend of hers who knows Chris and Reina recently spoke to Reina at the jail. He says that, before they were arrested, he had a visit with them at the Portofino Apartments. She says her friend,

Steve, is not sure if he wants to talk to me because of his criminal history, and he definitely does not want to testify at a trial. He tells her he never did see the kids except for little Chris, but might have some useful information.

I make arrangements with Carrie to meet at her house, so we can talk to Steve in person. I advise Sue, and we go over to Carrie's home and meet with Steve. He says he doesn't want the interview recorded and doesn't want to testify in court. When we speak with him, the information he provides is basically the same as what I initially received over the telephone, and that call was recorded. We never use him or require him to testify.

Day 74: Tuesday, May 2, 2007

After the death notifications have been made to Jamie and her family, I call and tell her that Chris and Reina have been arrested. I know I want stay in touch with her. Mike and I go to her house to see how she's doing. We do this because we feel that, even though she's addicted to drugs, she's not only fighting those demons, but is suffering the loss of her children.

We feel that the problems in her life don't matter, and she doesn't deserve what she's going through because her children were murdered at the hands of their father. We go to see her and, at first, she doesn't open the door. We're persistent, and she finally comes out. I see she's very thin and seems very depressed. She speaks softly when she greets us. She seems very shy and untrusting with us.

She does let us come in, and we tell her how sorry we are for her children. We tell her it appears that she's still using drugs and, for her children's sake, she needs to get off them. We tell her she needs to cooperate with CPS because they're thinking of taking custody of her five-month-old baby. She says she understands what we're saying, but it's difficult.

We tell her we're not here to judge her life or to say that what she's done is wrong. We tell her we feel that what happened to her kids is not her fault. We tell her she needs to trust us because there's still a lot of work to be done in this case. She says she understands what we're saying, and she'll try.

I meet with her several times on my own just to get her to trust me. I update her on what I can without compromising the investigation. We mainly speak about her kids and what they meant to her. I can tell her walls are breaking down, and she's beginning to trust me.

On a couple of occasions, I meet with Sue and drive over to Jamie's trailer. Sue also wants to gain Jamie's trust, not only for the trial, but also for the same reasons I have: concern and compassion for her and her family.

The first visit that Sue and I have with Jamie, Sue knocks on the door, and there's no answer. We're not sure if she's home or not. We go next door and speak to someone who's working on a truck. I ask him if he's seen Jamie. He tells me she's home, but is probably not answering the door.

Sue knocks again and, as she's doing that, I look around. I see Jamie hiding behind a small group of trees. I call to her and ask her to come over. Sue introduces herself and explains to Jamie her role in the prosecution of Chris and Reina, and what is to be expected. Jamie is reassured that we're there for her and sees that we'll do the best we can to seek justice for her children. Sue does a good job of talking to her. After the visit, I know Jamie is struggling. I'm not sure if she's going to be able to pull herself together.

Another time I meet Sue, and we drive to visit Jamie. After we finish, I'm driving us back to her office. Along the way, Sue begins to see how I feel about the investigation. I know she has concerns because the media is trying to get whatever information they can get their hands on. It seems that every day there's something in the news about the case. Sue is concerned because one of the commanders reported that we had searched the Dumpster, and Tyler's remains were not found.

Sue tells me she's concerned about a possible cover up, indicating that we did physically search the Dumpster when we actually didn't. I become somewhat angry and surprised, and tell her I would never do anything to compromise an investigation. I tell her that whatever happened at the scene is what I will testify to, and it doesn't matter to me what was reported. I tell her that, for me, there's only one way to conduct an investigation, and that's with honesty and integrity.

I tell her I would never want anyone to go to prison because an investigation was compromised, or allow anyone who is guilty to later on be set free by compromising an investigation. I explain to her that I feel guilty for not taking custody of the Dumpster and removing the debris and its contents. I tell her that the reason I didn't was because I never expected another body to be in the Dumpster, and we never even knew Tyler was part of this investigation until seven or eight days later.

I tell her it was my responsibility; I instinctively thought about it and should have done it. I also tell her that, as far as I knew, all the evidence was sitting on top of the debris in the Dumpster. This included the tub that had been removed, the lid that was taken out by TPD Crime Scene, and the contents of the tub itself.

I tell her that Ariana didn't have any clothes on at the time of discovery, and there was nothing to indicate that any paperwork linked to the discovery of Ariana's body was missing. I tell her we had the file from the office and the statement from Ms. Hanselman telling us what was in the storage unit and tub. I reassure Sue that I'm going to testify to the truth and nothing else. I also tell her I knew the question would come up at the trial as to why the Dumpster wasn't searched, and I will truthfully tell them why.

The media is also asking the same question, and deep down it bothers me that we haven't found Tyler's body. It's something I will have to live with the rest of my life. I feel from Sue a sigh of relief after talking to her about it. I believe she feels at ease and is comfortable talking to me about the investigation. To be quite honest, I'm a little surprised she would ask me about this. I've dealt with her on other cases and always thought she is very good at what she does. I really didn't get to know her until we worked together on this case. Several times we sat down and continued to put the pieces of the puzzle together.

I will say that, after working with Sue on this case, I've never seen anyone work as hard as she does. I found out that she is this way on all of her cases. She leaves no stone unturned and is relentless and driven. She reviews interviews over and over, and knows the law. In my opinion, she's the best the Pima County Attorneys Office has. I told a friend of mine that she could've won the O. J. Simpson case.

Day 80: Tuesday, May 8, 2007

I've been calling the University of North Texas Health Science Center in Ft. Worth once a week since early March. After about eight weeks, I finally receive the Forensic DNA report from them. The report contains the DNA profiles of Jamie Hallam, Christopher Payne, and Ariana Payne. The report states that Christopher and Jamie cannot be excluded as the biological parents of Ariana. It also states that, based on the DNA analysis and probability, the deceased child is Ariana Payne. I call Jamie and tell her. I send a copy of the letter to Sue and Bunkye's staff.

Day 82: Thursday, May 10, 2007

Donna is one of Chris's aunts from his stepmother's side. I call her and set up a meeting. Sue and I want to conduct an interview with her to see what she knows about Chris and Reina. After we arrive, I ask her if we can record the interview. She agrees, and we ask her about Chris and Reina. She provides us with the history on Chris and Reina. She also speaks about what he was like and his previous relationships. She tells us how difficult it was for her to deal with the deaths of Tyler and Ariana.

After the interview is concluded, we speak with Chris's step-sister, Julie. She also tells us the history on Chris and talks about his previous relationships and what he was like. She tells us about Tyler and Ariana, and how difficult it was dealing with their deaths. Julie tells me Chris wrote her a letter from jail. She says she could only read part of it because it made her upset.

She says she can't remember the specifics about what was said other than him approving of them taking care of little Chris. I ask her for the letter, and she says I can have it. I pick it up from her and later give her a copy of it, so she can finish reading it. She answers my questions and the interview is concluded.

Most of the history on Chris will come up in court, so I don't want to dwell on his childhood history. It does seem to me that the family is stunned by what took place and is having a difficult time dealing with it. After listening to the families, I notice a common theme: whenever anyone from either side of the family would ask about Tyler or Ariana, Chris and Reina would lie to them and tell them the kids were either with one of their friends or with other family members.

Day 83: Friday, May 11, 2007

I call Debbie and ask to meet with her to talk about Chris, Reina, and the children. After a time is arranged, Mike and I go over to her house and record the interview. She speaks about the history and relationships between Chris, Reina, the family, and the kids. It's pretty consistent with what everyone else has said, but she does disclose that she's received a few letters from Chris in jail. When I tell her I want them, she says I can keep the originals as long as I give her copies. (I come back at a later time with her copies.)

She tells us that her parents, Forrest and Pat, are moving back to Tucson and will arrive tomorrow. She answers the rest of our questions, and then the interview is concluded. After the letters are collected, they're placed into property as evidence, along with the other letter that was collected from Julie.

When we come back to the office, I call Old Pueblo Human Resources and speak with Christy Dotson. I advise her of the investigation and tell her I need the employment records for Reina Gonzales. She confirms that Reina was employed by Nicolisi & Fitch from 08/19/05 to 12/31/05, and employed by the Schomac Group from 01/01/06 to 01/31/06 as a leasing agent. A copy of her employment is faxed over to me. A copy is then placed into evidence as property, and a copy is sent over to PCAO (Pima County Attorney's Office).

Day 88: Wednesday, May 16, 2007

After several meetings with Sue and Bunkye, it's decided to add the murder charge of the Payne children to Reina. I meet with Pima County Attorney Bunkye Chi. The new charge is officially issued and later presented to the Grand Jury.

In Pima County, whenever a felony case is charged against a person, it has to be presented to the Pima County Attorney's Office. They will go over the case with all of the reports they've received and either accept or decline it. If they feel their needs to be more probable cause, then they will dismiss it for further investigation.

If the case gets accepted, then they can keep the charges as is, add charges, or pass it on to the Grand Jury, which can add charges if so decided. A preliminary hearing is also a possibility instead of a Grand Jury hearing.

Day 90: Friday, May 18, 2007

I present the case to the Grand Jury. I later discover that Reina was indicted. After receiving a copy of the warrant issued by the Grand Jury, I want to personally present this to Reina at the jail. I go over to the jail and meet with her. I tell her about the indictment and warrant. She doesn't say too much other than asking me to explain it to her. To me, she seems cold-hearted, and the news doesn't seem to faze her. I spend the rest of the day catching up on paperwork.

Day 94: Tuesday, May 22, 2007

I put in a medical records request for Tyler at the El Dorado Hospital. I find out that El Dorado Hospital no longer exists, and the old records are kept at Tucson Medical Center. I go to TMC Records and give them the request form. They later call me and tell me the requested records are ready, so I pick them up. If you're wondering about the HIPAA (Health Insurance Portability and Accountability Act) laws in the state of Arizona, they don't apply if you're conducting a child abuse investigation.

Day 95: Wednesday, May 23, 2007

I call Forrest Payne and ask to meet with him and his wife, Pat. I tell him I want to speak to them about Chris, Reina, and the children. A time is arranged, and Mike and I go over to their house to conduct a recorded interview.

The interviews are conducted separately, and we decide to speak to Pat first. She says they've recently moved back to Tucson from Virginia. She's asked about the history and relationships between Chris, Reina, the family, and the kids. She says Chris was her stepson; his mother, Socorro, passed away when he was only 18 months old. They did the best they could in raising Chris. She says he was okay at first, but did get into trouble with drugs in high school. She repeats that they did the best they could with him.

After speaking with her, Forrest is brought in. He confirms that, while they lived in Virginia, they would come down and vacation in Tucson for two weeks in February and work the Rodeo. He says they were here in February, but they didn't get a chance to see his grandchildren.

He says that, whenever he asked for them, he was always told they were either with other family members or friends. He says that, during last year, he did visit with Chris and the kids, and he recalls them as being healthy, well-dressed, and clean. He also tells us he helped Chris and Reina financially while he was here.

Both of them answer our questions and are visibly upset about what has happened to their grandchildren and to their son, Chris. Forrest says he feels Reina is also responsible for what has happened, and not Chris alone. He says she's the one who manipulated the relationship. He answers other questions, and the interview is concluded.

At first, I'm not sure what to think about the Paynes. I feel bad for them because of what has happened to their grandchildren. I know they're upset about it, but at the same time I can tell they're going to protect Chris as much as they can.

Day 97: Friday, May 25, 2007

I call Mirna Gonzales and ask to meet with her to speak about Chris, Reina, and the children. A time is arranged, and Mike and I go over to her house, where the interview is recorded. She speaks about what she knows of Chris, Reina, the family, and the kids. She answers our questions, and the interview is concluded.

Later in the day, I meet Sue at her office, and she tells me their office has decided to file a notice to Reina and her attorney that they will be seeking the death penalty. After reviewing the case, they met with her supervisors and agreed that Reina was just as responsible for the death of the children as Chris. The official paperwork is sent to Reina's attorneys advising them of the notice to seek the death penalty.

I'm pleased with the decision.

Day 125: Friday, June 22, 2007

I receive a call from Crime Lab DNA Analyst Nora Rankin. She tells me her report is finished. Part of the report states that 7BG-1 (the carpet padding with bloodstains taken from the bedroom closet) is the DNA profile from a male person and that Jamie Hallam and Christopher Payne cannot be excluded as the biological parents of this person. It is Tyler's DNA.

Day 181: Friday, August 17, 2007

One of the Homicide detectives calls me and tells me that an inmate, Juan Felix, wants to talk to the detectives about the Christopher Payne case, because he possibly has important information to disclose. Mike and I respond to the Pima County Jail and speak to him in one of the interview rooms. The interview is recorded.

He states that he's been speaking to Christopher through one of the vents, and feels he'll be able to get information on the case in exchange for a reduction on his charges. He's told we don't have the authority to make a deal with him. He says he really doesn't want to talk until he's gathered more information. We thank him and leave.

THE TRIAL

TYLER AND ARIANA PAYNE
CHRISTMAS DAY, 2005

The Attorneys

The court has appointed attorneys Rebecca McLean and Jack O'Brien to represent Chris. The court has appointed attorneys Brick Storts and Maria Davila to represent Reina. The attorneys for Chris and Reina will spend the next two years deciding on the defense strategy for their clients' cases. It's likely they will point the finger at each other and claim the other person was responsible for the death of these precious children.

Both Chris and Reina are facing the death penalty. There are two ways to be eligible to receive the death penalty in the State of Arizona. In one instance, you have to show intent that a person planned and proceeded to cause the death of another person. The other way is under the Felony Murder Rule, whereby a person's actions during the course of committing a crime cause the death of another. In this instance, the starvation and injuries these children sustained and their imprisonment in the closet caused their death. All of this was done in a heinous, depraved manner, so the death penalty is warranted.

During the first year after the arrests of Chris and Reina, there's not much activity from the attorneys. I know this is a complex case, and there are a lot of interviews, documents, and other paperwork that the attorneys have to go through.

What does happen during that year is that there are major changes in the Arizona CPS system. There have been numerous recent child murders involving kids in the foster system. CPS has failed to protect them and do the proper follow-up investigation on the children once they're placed in these homes. Changes in the system are now designed to hold CPS accountable for keeping track of the kids. They're required to work with law enforcement more directly and place the children in the safest environment possible.

It just happens that this case was the cornerstone for these changes because of how CPS failed these two kids.

Sometime over the summer of 2008, Reina decides to come forth with what happened to Tyler and Ariana. She tells Brick Storts' investigators, Leo Duffner and Joe Godoy, about her involvement and what happened to the kids in detail. We don't get this information until we receive a letter towards the end of July 2008.

Well, this triggers some legal maneuvering between Mr. Storts and Sue Eazer. Mr. Storts sends Sue a letter that Reina wants to "Free Talk," but in return she wants to strike a plea agreement. A "Free Talk" is when one person or arrestee has information to offer, but has accepted a plea offer in exchange for the information. The person is obligated to tell the truth, and if that person is found to be lying, then the plea offer will be dropped and the original charges given back, along with a contempt charge. Sue agrees to hear what Reina has to say, but does not offer a plea. (Later on, Reina is offered a plea of a 22-year prison-only term for the deaths of Tyler and Ariana, and no death penalty.)

A "Free talk" is set up with Reina, her attorneys, and the investigators. Sue, Bunkye, Pima County Attorney Investigator Irene Hazard, and I attend the "Free talk" at the Pima County Jail. It is recorded.

Reina discloses what we already know and have investigated. Tyler and Ariana were kept in the closet for long periods of time and were hardly fed. She goes on to say that Chris used the buckle of a belt and inflicted a wound on Tyler's head that was never treated.

Tyler suffered a cut and was placed in the closet, bleeding. He was never treated for the cut. She says the wound became infected because it turned green. She indicates that she was not close to the kids, and at one point wanted to send them back to Jamie. Chris didn't want to do this and kept the kids.

She further states that Debra Reyes and three other men spent about three months living with her and Chris. She says Debra and the other men were drug-dealing associates who, at the time, needed a place to stay. She says the kids were alive during that time, but were kept in the closet. Their associates never knew the kids were there. They stayed in the living room and never went into the closet or bedroom.

Reina tries to go into the dates and times that all this happened, but is confused (too much drug use). She says she never knew Ariana was hurt or injured.

After the "Free talk," it's decided to try and track down the additional persons that Reina has implicated in order to verify her information. During the next two to three months, PCAO investigator Irene Hazzard and I look for these people. We need to verify Reina's statement as much as we can. We're able to find some of the associates, but not all. The most compelling witness is Debra Reyes. We find out that she's still in the Pima County Jail, and we conduct an interview with her. She pretty much confirms what Reina told us, but the timelines are different as to when she and her associates were living with Chris and Reina.

The trial is set before Judge Richard Fields and is scheduled to begin January 27, 2009. Jack O'Brien and Rebecca McLean, the state-appointed attorneys representing Chris, file a continuance stating they need more time to prepare. Judge Fields grants them another three weeks to prepare. The trial is moved to February 17, 2009 for jury selection. This is almost two years to the day since we discovered the body of Ariana Payne.

You would think that after two years the defense would be ready. Mr. O'Brien also files a motion to suppress the statement that Chris gave to Mike and me. His statement was very damaging to his defense because of the confession he made about the kids and how they died while under his care. It also displayed his character, and how he looked at the time. The suppression hearing is set for January 22, 2009 in Judge Fields' courtroom.

Prior to the hearing, I want to know what I'm up against with Mr. O'Brien. I ask several attorneys and staff from the Pima County Attorneys Office what he's like as a defense attorney. I'm told he's very meticulous, thorough, and aggressive. I'm also told that he objects a lot in court and files countless motions.

Friday, January 16, 2009

A defense interview is scheduled, and I'm well versed in my reports and know my case. I feel that I'm prepared enough when I go into the interview. My interview is broken up into two separate days, totaling about five or six hours. The second part of the interview is set for January 23, 2009.

The first interview lasts about three to four hours and, when I'm finished, my confidence is somewhat shaken because I feel I didn't do as well as expected. Mr. O'Brien challenges me by going through my reports, page by page, and asks me questions that are, at times, difficult to answer. Some things are hard to remember. It was, after all, two years ago that we investigated this case. The reports are reminders of the work you did and how the whole investigation came together. So there were times I couldn't recall certain events. Though they were minor, O'Brien played them up.

Bunkye Chi is there during my interview, and afterward I ask her how I did. She tells me I did okay, but I need to be more confident regarding our investigation, and present that confidence in court. I listen to her, and I know I need to step up and really study my case. But I did get through the interview.

I want to win the suppression hearing, and I ask Bunkye on several occasions how they feel about winning it. She says she doesn't feel we'll win, but she'll fight for it. She says the defense is presenting two issues regarding Chris's statement. One is Miranda, and the other is the volunteerism of the statement.

She says that, after Miranda was read to him, he stated several times he didn't want to talk to Mike, but he was still questioned. He not only did that with Mike, but also with other officers. Mr. O'Brien is also challenging the fact that Chris was going through heroin withdrawal and is making it an issue that Chris was not coherent enough to give a fair statement. She says they feel that, if they lose the statement, they still have enough evidence to convict Chris. I feel better about this and am more confident.

Friday, January 23, 2009

Mr. O'Brien and Ms. McLean want to view the collected evidence and request a viewing. It's set for 10:00 a.m. at the TPD evidence building. Sue, Bunkye, Mike, and I meet with Mr. O'Brien and Ms. McLean. As part of disclosure, the defense has a right to view any collected evidence, and they can also request copies of any documents. We spend the next couple of hours viewing them, piece-by-piece. Numerous item requests are made for getting them copied. I later give them the requested copies.

One important note I want to pass on is that, when the original tub is brought out for the viewing, the horrible smell of death still emanates from the tub and other items. It's almost overpowering. The defense attorneys cover their noses, trying to avoid the smell, but it obviously doesn't help. I'm happy that the defense has shared in the horrid smell, so they can see what their clients have done to these kids. The smell was much worse at the scene.

After this, I finish the other part of my interview with Mr. O'Brien. It's now time for the hearing and trial. I will be prepared.

The Hearing & Ruling

Thursday – Monday, January 22 – 26, 2009

It's time for the hearing and, as the lead detective, you're allowed to sit with the prosecution and not be part of the exclusionary rule. The 'exclusionary rule' means that any witnesses or potential witnesses are not allowed in the courtroom during the proceedings, so they won't be influenced in any way prior to their testimony.

When you're a witness, any testimony you give should come from what you remember. When you can't remember, you can be reminded through any recorded, written, or transcribed statements, but preferably through the transcribed statements. No hearsay testimony is allowed in a criminal trial (although it is in civil trials).

What is discussed between the judge and attorneys is what will be allowed into the trial. Any prior criminal acts have to be filed for admission. Domestic Violence history is usually not allowed, along with other issues that they agree upon ahead of time. This is done to make this a fair trial, one not prejudicial to the defendant. This is why the public doesn't always hear all the evidence, or understand that some testimony or evidence is not presented at the trial.

The motion hearing starts with the defense and prosecution presenting their cases. All of the officers testify, and the state does a wonderful job of showing how Chris was in control and manipulating the interviews. The video displays how, each time there was a crossroad in the interview or the interview was about to end, Chris would re-initiate contact and ask to continue to talk.

After both prosecution and defense have presented their cases, Judge Fields takes the case under advisement. Judge Fields takes about a week to review the video and refer to the law enforcement officers' testimony. I feel the ruling will go in our favor.

During the week we spend waiting for Judge Fields to make his ruling, I speak to Mike about the proceedings and tell him how I feel. During the waiting phase, Mike has an issuing case with Bunkye. He tells her I think we have a good chance of winning this decision. She takes it as somewhat of a joke that I would really believe we could win it. It's the prosecution's opinion that we will lose this. They believe that, because Chris stated several times during the interview that he did not want to talk, his Miranda rights were violated. Now, I'm not an attorney, but I think the fact that he never asked for a lawyer during the interview makes a big difference. I personally think we have a very good shot at winning this ruling.

Mike comes back from her office and tells me what she's said. I tell him I disagree with her. It doesn't bother me what she's said, because she knows the law and the court proceedings. Obviously, she's seen this before and has a different outlook on it than I do. It's her opinion.

I tell Mike that the prosecutors are too involved in their presentation to the court to see how it appears to someone watching and listening on the outside. I was there throughout all of the proceedings. I tell Mike that, from my point of view, I agree with the way Sue and Bunkye presented their case, showing how Chris tried to manipulate and control the interviews and contacts. Mike says he's not sure how it will go. I know our case will be that much stronger if the judge rules in our favor.

The following is the official ruling by Judge Fields, and the foundation for his findings. The prosecutors did a great job of presenting the case.

Arizona Superior Court, Pima County
Judge: Hon. Richard S. Fields
Court Reporter: N/A
Case No: 2007-0973
Date: February 4th 2009

State of Arizona, Plaintiff

Vs.

Christopher Matthew Payne, Defendant

RULING

UNDER ADVISEMENT RULING

Procedural History

The court has under advisement Defendants Motion to Suppress. The action arises from an indictment on Mr. Payne March 12th 2007, for two-counts of First Degree Murder, a Class One Felony and seven other counts relating to Mr. Payne's two children.

On December 18th 2007 Mr. Payne, by and through Counsel filed a motion to suppress statements. The state responded on January 7th 2009. Defense counsel filed a motion to suppress on January 15th 2009. The state responded on January 21st 2009. A hearing was held on January 22nd 2009 and completed on January 26th 2009.

The defense argues that the defendant's statements should be suppressed because they were made involuntarily and in violation of Miranda. The state argues that the statements were voluntary with no violation of Miranda.

Facts

On March 1st 2007, Detectives Orozco and Walker of the Tucson Police Department responded to the Lazy 8 motel where the defendant and his girlfriend were staying. The detectives approached the room where the defendant and his girlfriend were staying and made contact with the two individuals. The defendant then asked the officers what was happening. Detective Orozco advised him they were conducting an investigation and he, the defendant might have information. The defendant refused a request to go downtown with the officers and Detective Orozco then served him with an outstanding warrant and placed him into custody.

The defendant is then transported to the Main Police Station, 270 S. Stone and Reina and her son, Chris Jr. follow. When the defendant arrives he is placed in an interview room where he speaks to several officers and two detectives. During this period the defendant admitted that Tyler and Ariana died while under his care.

Suppression

During a custodial interrogation, once a suspect of a criminal investigation has invoked his right to have counsel present for the questioning, all the questioning must stop. *Edwards vs. Arizona, 451, US, 477 (1981); citing in part Miranda vs. Arizona, 384, US, 486, 469-73 (1966).* Custodial Interrogation is described as "questioning initiated by law enforcement officers after a person has been taken into custody or otherwise deprived of his freedom of action in any significant way." *Miranda 384 US at 444.*

Whether custodial interrogation has taken place is an objective test based on whether a reasonable person would feel that he or she was deprived of his or her freedom in any significant way. *State vs. Hatton, 116 Arizona, 142, 146 (1977), State vs. Wyman 10, 13 (appx. 2000).*

02/04/2009

T. Clayton Kamm
Law Clerk

Ruling
Date: 02/04/2009   CR: 2007-0973

If an ambiguous or equivocal request for counsel has been made, Arizona courts have held that questioning does not need to stop and questioning may continue on any topic. *See State vs. Eastlack, 180 Arizona 243, 250-51(1994); State vs. Finehout, 136 Arizona, 226, 229 (1983).*

Statements made after an invocation of a right to counsel have been made will not be suppressed if voluntarily, knowingly, and intelligently made. *Edwards 451 US 477 (1981)*

In *Edwards* the police arrested the defendant and informed him of his rights, *Id at 478*. Edwards then waived his right to counsel and proceeded to confess his guilt to the police, *id*. However, before he spoke to the county attorney, he informed the officers that he "want[ed] an attorney" before making a deal, *id 479*.

The following day, a detention officer informed the defendant that two detectives wanted to speak to him, *id*. The defendant told the officer that he did not wish to speak with anyone to which the officer replied that "he had" to, *id*. The detention officer brought the defendant to the detectives, *id*. The detectives then Mirandized the defendant, and then the defendant gave his confession to the detectives, *id*.

The court held that while the defendant's second waiver of his right to counsel was voluntary, it was not intelligently and knowingly made, *id. at 484-86*. The court noted that one example of a voluntary, intelligent, and knowingly made confession would be one where the defendant self-initiates the dialogue between him or herself and the officers, *id. 485*.

Statements made after a suspect has been Mirandized must be made voluntarily. *State vs. Griffin, 148 Arizona 82, 85 (1986).* "Confessions are prima facie involuntary and burden is on the State to show a confession was freely and voluntarily made." *State vs. Knapp, 114 Arizona 531, 539.* However, the question of

Volunteerism relies to a great extent on the actions of the interrogating police officers, e.g. whether there is evidence of police coercion. *Colorado vs. Connelly, 479 US 157, 170 (1986); State vs. Bravo, 158 Arizona 364, 370 (Ariz. App. 1988)*

The Supreme Court stated, "Coercive police activity is a necessary predicate to the finding that a confession is not 'voluntary' within the meaning of the Due Process Clause of the Fourteenth Amendment." *Connelly, 479 US at 167.* Using *Connelly* the Arizona Supreme Court stated that not withstanding a blood alcohol level of .22 the defendant's statements were voluntary because there was no evidence that the officers "threatened, intimidated, or deceived" the defendant. *State vs. Tucker, 157 Ariz. 433, 445-46 (1988).*

This Court also notes that mental illness will not render a statement involuntary "unless the illness renders the declarant unable to understand the meaning of the statements made." *State vs. Bravo, 158 Arizona 364, 370 (Ariz. App. 1988); citing State vs. Porter, 122 Ariz. 453, 456 (1979).*

However, the Arizona Supreme Court has also noted that while intoxication and mental illness do not render a statement involuntary, the court must look to the "totality of the circumstances to determine 'whether police conduct constituted overreaching'." *State vs. Smith, 193 Ariz. 452, 457 (1999).*

This court has pondered the arguments of counsel, considered all of the authorities cited and spent about twelve to fifteen hours analyzing the *Miranda-Edwards* issue in this case. It is only at this junction of the law that the decision becomes difficult.

Volunteerism is an easy call in this case. Mr. Payne proved to be a strong-willed intelligent negotiator with Det. Walker. He made demands; he tried to extract benefits via promises to 'tell all'. He gave, he threatened to withhold. When one strategy did not work he undertook others.

While Mr. Payne <u>may</u> have been experiencing some discomfort in the form of withdrawal symptoms, his will was far from being overborne. His attempt to extract promises was the earmark of a negotiator from the school of hard knocks and the streets, not that of an eggshell defendant about to be pushed over the edge by unsolicited police promises. The voluntary aspect of Defendant's statements to Detectives on March 1, 2007 was exemplified in an exchange that took place on Bates Stamp Page 101213, on Defendant's exhibit "A":

A: [Payne]: I don't remember man, I been scared (sniffles). This weighed on my conscience more that anything. Why do you think I opened up to this guy right here?
Q: [Orozco]: Um-um (affirmative response)
A: It needed to come out.
*****(Omitted sentences)
A: the fucking (f) shit was eaten (ph) me alive man. I coulda sat here and clammed up, (unknown noise in the background) you know.

Mr. Payne was willing and eager to talk to the police, corrections officers, anyone who would listen to his perspective on why things happened the way they did. This concluded statements to Corrections Officer Medina, Officer Lemas, Officer Parish and Payne's sister, Debbie Barbone.

Alas it also applies to Detective Walker and Orozco. Now this court would be remiss if it did not point out to the detective herein that the best way to have proceeded in the instant case was to be certain that any earlier statements about attorneys was conveyed to all before contact was made at the main station. Any doubts could have been put to bed and this court has absolutely no doubt that, following a few attempts to extract promises, Mr. Payne would have quickly assured Det. Walker as he later did with Orozco: "Don't need a lawyer man. Let's rock dude!"

This court cannot ignore the overwhelming factual context surrounding the initial statement to Det. Orozco and the later defendant-initiated conversation at the main police station at 270 S.

Stone. On March 1, 2007 the defendant and his girlfriend (Reina Gonzales) were at the Lazy 8 Motel and were approached by Det. Orozco. [M.O.: This is the legal matter I mentioned when we first approached Chris at the Lazy 8 Motel.]

The defendant was advised that the police were conducting an investigation and thought that the defendant might have some information. The Detective then asked if the defendant would be willing to "come downtown and talk to us at the police station." *Direct of Orozco testimony at 7.* At this time the defendant stated, "I'm not going downtown without my lawyer." *Id.*

The court notes that the mention of an attorney was made before the officers had arrested the defendant and before any formal or informal interrogation or custody had taken place. Payne now knew that he was no longer alone. The detectives wanted Payne to play an 'away' game. He said no. He was not in custody. He was asked to go downtown and he didn't want to. This was not an ambiguous invocation of the right to counsel.

To determine if a violation of *Edwards vs. Arizona* occurred, this court focuses on statements Payne made to an unidentified police officer and Det. Walker on March 1, 2007. Analysis of this interaction demonstrates Payne's voluntary, knowingly, and intelligently made waiver of his right to counsel.

The transcripts of the interviews provide us with numerous examples where the defendant demands to talk to Walker and control the discussion. The following exchange occurs immediately after Mr. Payne is first brought into the holding room:

A: All right, tell these guys I ain't gonna (ph) answer no questions unless they hurry the fuck up, man.

The court notes that this is an indication of self-initiation that cannot be overlooked. Later when Det. Walker arrives the following dialogue occurs:

Q: Well, you're here for ah (ph) warrant, okay and we're conducting an investigation like we told you earlier…, and we'd like to (ph) ask you some questions.

A: All right well you're the only person I'll talk to, let's get talkin' (ph) right now.

Q: You gotta (ph) give me (2) seconds, okay; I gotta (ph) get organized.

A: Well, no, I'm not gonna (ph)

Q: You wanna (ph) do this right?

A: I'm not, I'm not gonna (ph) talk then eh (ph), if it's not gonna (ph) be right now.

Q: Okay.

A: *So let's talk* (emphasis added)

Q: You wanna (ph) talk right now?

A: Yeah, what's goin' (ph) on boss?

Not only does the defendant indicate his willingness to speak, he demands that this occur before Det. Walker is ready. Walker had entered to calm the defendant down, not to question him. Immediately after this occurred, Det. Walker informed the defendant of his Miranda rights and the Defendant, at that time, waived them. The Defendant initiated the discussion of the case. Any later refusals to talk were really only manipulation attempts. This court finds no violation of *Miranda or Edwards*.

This court is well aware that this decision will be reviewed in detail. Nevertheless, after watching five plus hours of defendant's interaction with other human beings, including the law enforcement officers, this court concludes that the Motion To Suppress Statements must be, in totality, DENIED, IT IS SO ORDERED.

Hon. Richard S. Fields

Now we are even more prepared for trial.

The Trial

Tuesday, February 17, 2009

The trial begins with questionnaires that are sent to a pool of potential jurors. These questionnaires are unique in the fact that the prosecution, defense, and judge get together and agree upon certain questions that pertain to the death penalty. Obviously, a person has to believe in the death penalty in order to be considered. I did not see or read the questionnaires that were sent out, but during the 'Voir Dire' (paneling of jurors) these questions were brought up.

There are other questions that have to be considered by a juror. That person has to know if they can pass judgment on a person and send them to their death. It's one thing to believe in the death penalty, but it's another to actually send someone to their death if they're convicted in a court of law. Some people cannot do this and do not want that person's fate in their hands.

Other questions take into consideration people who believe in the death penalty only for certain crimes. This case is a perfect example of that. These are just some of the issues brought up and questions asked, and I see the hesitation and uncertainty when these issues are presented to the jurors. Another question that's asked is how they feel about the judicial system.

What's sad is the number of jurors who are excused because someone they knew or someone related to them was murdered, and the murderer is now out of prison after serving their time.

They obviously believe the system has failed them, and rightfully so. It doesn't seem right that the system should fail them, but this is the system we have, and you cannot give up on it.

In a death penalty case, the prosecution and defense question each juror individually, rather than as a group. Once twenty-six jurors have been selected, each side gets ten strikes against any juror they don't want in the trial. Sixteen jurors are finally selected. Four jurors are to be randomly picked as alternates once the state and defense have rested their cases. These jurors are still part of the trial and have to listen to the proceedings. The first week is nothing but jury selection. It's difficult and at times tedious.

Mr. O'Brien and Ms. McLean are up to their antics, more so him than her. They grill each juror on how they answered their questionnaires and about the death penalty issues. At one time, Mr. O'Brien asks to have all of the jurors videotaped, so he can see their reactions to the questioning and base his selection on that. Judge Fields denies this motion and tells him it would not be reasonable.

They go through two groups of jurors, but the jury is finally selected, and it has taken the full week to pick them. On the final Friday of the selection process, we're supposed to leave the courthouse at 5:00 p.m., but instead we continue until 7:30 p.m. to get the jury finalized.

Ten men and six women are selected. Judge Fields has to admonish the jury at one point. What this means is that there are specific instructions the jurors have to follow according to what the judge, the prosecution, and the defense have agreed to previously.

The most important instruction the judge imposes on the jury is that they have to avoid any media coverage. They're also instructed not to speak to anyone about the case, and not to listen to anyone speaking or conversing about it. They are instructed to take good notes, but not to discuss the case with any of their fellow jurors until deliberations.

Each juror is given a binder with notepads, pencils, and the instructions. Each juror sits in an assigned chair and is known by a number rather than a name. All of the jurors are told they'll be dismissed by the judge every day and will probably be off for the weekend or any other time that the judge feels is necessary. Hopefully, they'll get plenty of rest to gear up for the actual trial, which is due to start with opening statements on Monday morning.

What's also important to know is that whoever has the burden of proof in a trial, whether the defense or prosecution, gets to present a final rebuttal after each side presents their opening statement. Usually, the State is first to present their opening statement, because they have the burden of proof in a criminal trial. The Defense then presents its opening statement, and afterward the State gets a final rebuttal.

Day 1: Wednesday, February 25, 2009

To my surprise, Bunkye Chi is the first to present the case to the court (I thought Sue would be the one to start out). She is gracious and direct. She first speaks of Tyler and Ariana and presents an emotional slide show on the short lives of the kids. It has a direct effect. The courtroom is quiet, and some of the jurors get emotional when they see the children and realize they've been murdered. She then moves toward speaking about Chris and how evil he is. She is tenacious.

She tells the jury that Chris minimally fed the kids to the point where they were near starvation. She says he didn't feed them due to lack of money, because they always had plenty of money for their heroin habit. She describes how Ariana's tiny body was placed in a trash bag, then stuffed into a Tommy Hilfiger canvas bag, and then into a Rubbermaid storage tub. Tyler's body was also placed in the tub, but was not found inside the tub with Ariana.

Ariana's body was discovered only after Chris and Reina stopped making payments to the storage facility. After the manager could no longer stand the smell of the decomposing body in the tub, she decided to place the tub in the Dumpster. The manager called a friend, told her about the horrible smell, and said she had discarded the tub in the Dumpster. The friend then advised her to call the police. The police responded and the investigation began.

She states that it was approximately a week later before the police found out about Tyler. She says his blood was later found in the bedroom closet where Chris and Reina were living. The smell there was overwhelming from the decomposition of the bodies that had been at the apartment.

Months later, the smell still lingers in the apartment after the children's bodies have been moved. It's still very difficult to get rid of the smell. The extent of decomposition on Ariana's body was so drastic that a formal autopsy could not be done. An anthropologist had to step in and forensically examine the remains of her body.

What was discovered in the remains were extensive injuries with different stages of healing in the broken bones. Ariana had numerous fractured ribs consistent with her being picked up and squeezed out of anger. She also had a broken shoulder consistent with some type of impacted trauma, possibly from a fall, and a compressed vertebra or broken back.

She goes on to say that Chris and Reina had a child together, and it was evident there was a difference in how they cared for him versus how they cared for Ariana and Tyler. Their child was healthy, well fed, and developmentally within the normal range of children his age. She says that sightings of Tyler and Ariana became less and less frequent. When family asked about the kids, Chris and Reina lied to them as to their whereabouts.

When Ariana died, Chris and Reina "freaked out" and got high to numb their pain. After they were finally found and detained, they lied to the police. Later on, Chris was interrogated and said the kids starved themselves and had "quit" on him by not eating. Chris then came up with a plan to conceal their remains, so he could continue with his life with Reina and their son.

She says that, after the kids died, they were then kept inside the outside storage closet of the apartment until Chris and Reina decided to move them to the U-Store-It facility. They were then placed in storage unit #C19. She continues to cover the highlights of the investigation, from the time of the discovery at the storage room to the gruesome remains of Ariana. She moves on and, after she is done, the courtroom is quiet.

The defense team then gets their turn. Rebecca McLean makes their opening statement. She tries to portray Chris as a caring and loving father who was caught up into drugs, and blames the death of his children on Reina Gonzales. She says Chris loved his children and did not abuse them, and that Reina hated the children and was the one who wanted them dead.

She says Jamie Hallam was a bad mother who was addicted to methamphetamines. Chris took the children to get them out of that environment and felt he could take better care of them. She says Jamie was uncooperative with CPS and had been investigated by them. Ms. McLean was pushing this, because she was not allowed by the court to get into details about those allegations.

She says that, when Tyler was two years old, he was taken to the doctor and, after being examined, he was found to be underweight. Ariana was also taken to a doctor at two years old, was diagnosed as having high levels of lead in her system, and was given a prescription for "psychological" reasons and for being in a suspected "abusive environment."

She says that Chris quit his job in 2004 to be a stay-at-home dad to his son with Reina. In 2005 Chris got a job with a medical transportation service. Afterward, he heard that Jamie was abusing drugs and, because of that, he wanted to spend more time with Tyler and Ariana.

Chris claims that, in January 2006, Jamie left the kids with him. He says that when they were dropped off they were underweight, dirty, and badly dressed. Ms. McLean says that, after they arrived, Reina couldn't stand having the children in their home and didn't want them around. She says Reina would constantly call Chris while he was at work and complain about the kids. She would at times yell at him and demand that he come home to take care of them.

Ms. McLean goes on to say that Chris was involved with drugs, and his boss at the transportation service suspected it because of his erratic behavior. He was eventually terminated, so afterward Chris began to sell drugs. She says that, even during the time Chris was working by selling drugs, Reina would yell and scream for him to come home and take care of his kids. She says that Reina would deny them juice and limit the amount of food they could have.

She says that Reina accepted a plea offer from the state and pleaded to 2nd degree murder, so she has admitted to being responsible for their deaths. She says that, after Ariana died, Chris was so upset he performed CPR on her most of the day and slept with her in the same bed, just to be with her. She says that, after Tyler died, Reina just wanted to throw their bodies away. Chris couldn't do that, so he initially put both of them in the tub and put the tub in the storage unit.

She also says the defense will provide medical evidence that the fractures on Ariana were present before the kids were given to Chris. The defense rests on the opening statements.

These are the highlights of the opening statements. The reason I'm providing them is because they set the tempo of the trial and introduce what will be attacked and defended by both defense and prosecuting attorneys.

What you should know is that the order of witnesses to testify gets changed a couple of times as the trial progresses. The witness testimonies as shown here are close to the days I remember. The trial also progresses as I remember it. Important events and witnesses are highlighted as the trial progresses.

The state first calls Diane Hanselman, the manager of the U-Store-It business. After she answers general questions from Sue, she goes into the protocols of renting a unit from the business. She states that she's not the one who rented unit #C19 to Mr. Neuser, but she was the person who managed all of the units. She says the unit was rented in September 2006 to Joshua Neuser.

She says the payments stopped coming after a month or so, and letters were sent out to him on defaults. After not hearing from him or receiving any payments, she placed an over-lock on the unit. After no one responded to the defaults, the auctioneers came to do an inventory of the unit.

She cut the owner's lock and went inside to conduct an inventory. The auctioneers smelled the awful odor and saw what was inside and decided to leave it alone. A picture was taken with a Polaroid camera. The over-lock was put back on the door. The next time she checked was on February 10, 2007. She went in, and the floor was crawling with insects. She thought it was strange and swept them out. She says the smell was terrible, and she thought there was a dead animal inside the tub. After she swept out the unit, she locked it up again. The next time she went in was on February 16. She said that was when she decided to throw out the tub. She put it on the cart and drove it over to the Dumpster.

She says it was awkward, and the lid twisted, but was still on the tub. She says she could see the canvas bag near the top of the tub. She remembers the terrible smell, and that some of the liquid spilled onto her shoe. She lifted the tub up to her shoulder and tipped it over into the Dumpster. She thought that the tub was half full and weighed about 45 pounds.

After dumping the tub, she left it in there, and for the next two days she contemplated what she should do. She was really bothered by the smell, and finally decided to call a friend of hers who is a paramedic living in Texas. Her friend told her to call the police, just to make sure it was an animal and not something else.

On Sunday, February 18, she decided to call the police, and the gruesome discovery was made. Diane grows emotional while describing the handling of the tub and placing it in the Dumpster. The courtroom is quiet, and the state rests.

The defense now has their turn to question Diane. It's pretty uneventful, but they do ask her about her duties, and who was around at the time the storage unit was rented. She's asked if she met or knew the person who rented it. Diane states that another employee rented the unit to Joshua Neuser, and she never met him. They don't seem to have a lot of questions to ask at this point.

Officer Ben Soltero is the next one called to testify. He states that at the time he was a rookie in training, and he goes into detail about the call. He states that when he arrived at the business he spoke with Ms. Hanselman. After getting an update from her, he was directed to the Dumpster with the tub inside. He pulled the tub out and opened up the Tommy Hilfiger bag and the plastic garbage bag inside.

Once he checked the contents inside, he saw the decomposing body of what appeared to be a child. He stepped back, left the tub where he had placed it, and secured the scene. He then notified his training officer. Their sergeant was then called, and the other notifications were then made to the commanders and detectives.

The defense council does not ask many questions on redirect.

OME Anthropologist, Dr. Bruce Anderson, is then called to testify. He states that he received the information about Ariana's remains from Dr. Erik Peters. He says Dr. Peters needed him to examine these remains because of the advanced stage of decomposition. He says that Dr. Peters could not complete the full autopsy because all of the organs had liquefied, and all that was left were the skin, bones, and teeth.

Dr. Anderson testifies that, after processing the remains, he was able to determine that Ariana had sustained eleven broken ribs, posterior and anterior, that had been healing. He says she also had sustained a broken shoulder and a broken back. He says the broken vertebrae could have occurred when she was placed inside the tub.

He goes on to say that the broken ribs and shoulder were from impacted trauma. He states that the bones had been healing for anywhere from six to eight weeks. He goes on to explain the healing process, the stages that bones go through while healing, and the remodeling stage that it takes for them to completely heal. He explains this very clearly, and it appears that the jurors understand the process.

The defense tries to dispute his findings on their rebuttal. They have their own expert witness who is going to testify that his timeline is inaccurate, and that the trauma to the bones occurred eight to twelve months earlier. Their theory is that Ariana sustained the injuries when she was with Jamie, not with Chris.

This concludes the first day at the courthouse.

Day 2: Thursday, February 26, 2009

There's a mixup in the order of witnesses scheduled to testify. Professor Carl Olsen, the entomology expert at the University of Arizona, was initially scheduled to testify, but he doesn't show up. He's contacted by one of the legal secretaries. He tells her he didn't know he was supposed to be in court, but will get down there as soon as he can. What happened is the legal secretary never notified him as to when he was supposed to appear in court.

Joshua Neuser is the next person called in to testify. He's obviously very nervous, but it should be taken into account that he's a heroin addict and alcoholic. He's a thin person who has trouble remembering details. He admits to being addicted to heroin and says he mainly uses enough just to "stay well." This is a term used by addicts, which means they use just enough heroin to keep functioning on a daily basis.

He does okay testifying and remembers renting the storage unit for Chris. He explains how Mike and I found him living at his mother's house, and how he agreed to come down to the police department for questioning. He remembers being placed in a holding cell and being questioned.

He remembers that his friend, Sandra Glazier, was also brought in for questioning. He remembers getting upset when he was told about the remains of a little girl being found. He says he never went into the storage unit and didn't know what was inside. He says he never paid rent on the unit. At the time, he can't remember the names of Chris and Reina.

The defense doesn't hammer him too much, but does press his inability to remember facts in detail.

After this questioning, the judge excuses everyone for lunch.

Professor Carl Olsen is the next one called to testify. Sue asks Professor Olsen about his credentials and expertise in the field of entomology. His answers show he's very qualified in his field. He's then asked about the insects I collected from the scene at the storage unit and the scene at the Portofino Apartments.

He states that the insect pupae were from the same species and were essentially flesh-eating larvae or flies, once they hatched. He states that the samples I gave him were exoskeletons. This means that the insect cases were empty because bugs had hatched, leaving them empty. He describes how they evolve, and the time it takes them to evolve.

He speaks about how they can get to the bodies through very small openings. He says that the plastic bag containing the body was probably not sealed all the way, so the insects managed to get in through the opening.

After he answers some questions by the defense, he's excused.

Braulio Gomez is the next witness to be called. He's the landfill truck driver, who picked up the trash for the U-Store-It business. He's familiar with the landfill operations and knows the area where he dumped the trash. He states that he advised the police of the area, but knew that finding anything specific would be a problem because of the extensive piling of trash and how spread out it was on top of an area that was continuously piled upon.

Not too many questions were asked by the defense.

Jamie Hallam is the next person to be called to testify. Jamie does a wonderful job of testifying. Sue starts her out with general questions. Jamie speaks about her relationship with Chris: when they met, had the kids, and then their divorce. Sue then moves toward asking her about her relationship with the kids. Jamie tells the court how wonderful they were, and how Tyler always seemed to protect his little sister.

She describes their personalities and how innocent and loving they were. She says Tyler loved to play with his trucks and was a finicky eater who did not like to eat meat. She says Ariana loved to color and dress up. She would always top off her outfit with her favorite baseball cap.

She goes on to say that the last time she saw her children was on January 20, 2006. She drove the children to their father for a week-end visit. She says the kids were excited to see their little brother (little Chris). After that weekend, Chris asked for an extended stay with the kids, because he wanted to take them to a birthday party. Jamie allowed it.

Chris then asked for another extended stay because of a Super Bowl party they were going to. She also allowed this visit. Jamie says that, after the last visit, Chris called her and told her he was not going to return the kids because he found out that CPS was investigating her.

Jamie says that, over the next month, she kept in contact with CPS, and on March 1, 2006, CPS told her their investigation was over, and that it was unsubstantiated and closed. She then tried to contact Chris to let him know she wanted her kids back. He never communicated with her again.

Jamie says she found out where Chris lived and called the Tucson Police Department to assist her in getting her kids back. She met them in the area of the Portofino Apartments. After she showed the officers the custodial orders, they went up to the apartment to investigate. They came back and advised her that CPS told them to leave the kids with Chris, because she was still under investigation.

She then tried to find out from CPS what was going on, but couldn't get any straight answers from them. She says that, during the continuing months, she had another baby and continued to use meth.

She says that Tucson Police Detectives contacted her in February 2007 and asked her for a DNA sample. She didn't know why until later, when they told her that Ariana was dead and that Tyler was also presumed to be dead.

Sue asks Jamie how she would discipline the kids whenever they misbehaved. She says she would give them timeouts or take-aways and never hit them. She says that neither of the kids ever had any falls or accidents where they sustained any broken bones. Sue asks her other questions and then finishes up.

Rebecca McLean does the cross-examination for the defense. She asks Jamie about the relationships she had before and after her relationship with Chris. She says that there was domestic violence, and that CPS did investigate her before Chris came into her life and after they were divorced. She says CPS was concerned about the DV and her drug use.

Jamie says she hasn't used meth in over two years, and she's clean. She also testifies that she filed a lawsuit against CPS and settled out of court for $1,000,000.00 in connection with her children's deaths. This concludes her testimony for the day. She is not excused as a witness and can be called upon again to testify.

Officer Bill Nutt is called to the stand. He testifies that on March 9, 2006 he was the officer who responded to the Portofino Apartments and investigated the custodial issue between Jamie Hallam and Christopher Payne. He states that he did meet with Jamie, and she told him she had full custody of her children and wanted them back. He says she also showed him court-ordered paperwork verifying that she had legal custody of the children.

He states that he went to Christopher's apartment and spoke to him. Chris was told of the court orders that Jamie had with her. Chris then told him he was seeking to modify the custody orders and was in the process of filling out the paperwork. He also told Officer Nutt that Jamie was under investigation by CPS for drugs.

Officer Nutt then called CPS and was told by them that there was an open case on Jamie and to leave the children with Chris. Officer Nutt further testifies that the children appeared to be happy, healthy, that the apartment was clean, and there was food in the refrigerator. Officer Nutt is the last witness to testify for the day.

The jury is excused first, and then everyone else.

What is also important to know is that there's a lot of legal maneuvering between the defense and prosecuting attorneys. The defense is constantly objecting to the line of questioning by the prosecution and wants them to either rephrase the question or properly ask it without prejudicing their client. I will say that the judge overruled most of the objections by the defense.

At times, I would look over at the jurors, and it would seem to me that they would get annoyed at the tedious objections. I realize that, in this case, the defense has their back against the wall. They're trying the only way they know how to convince the jurors to find their client guilty of the lesser charge, not the first degree murder and/or death penalty.

Day 3: Friday, February 27, 2009

I'm called to testify. After being sworn in, Sue asks me my name, where I work, the years I've been in law enforcement, the unit I'm currently assigned to, and how long I've been in the unit. She also asks me about my qualifications and the number of homicides I've worked. I answer all of her questions, but tell her I don't have a total on the number of homicides I've investigated.

She then asks me the standard questions about receiving the call and responding to the U-Store-It business, and if it was located in Pima County in the City of Tucson. I tell her I received the call from my supervisor, Sgt. Carlos Valdez, and that the business is located in Pima County and in the City of Tucson. After that, she begins by asking me what I did when I first arrived at the scene, and I describe what took place after I arrived at the U-Store-It.

Sue then asks me what I did next. I tell her that, after a briefing with everyone, it was decided I would process the crime scene and interview Ofc. Soltero. Det. Walker was assigned to gather the rental storage information from the manager and conduct an interview with her and any other possible witnesses. Sgt Valdez was basically overseeing the investigation and would be there for any support that we possibly needed.

Sue has decided to do a crime scene presentation with the photographs taken at the scene. This is now viewed by projecting the images onto a TV screen. We go through the pictures, and I explain in detail the crime scene and what we were looking for and why.

I tell the court we always have the scene photographed first to show how it is before we go in and begin our investigation. TPD CSS was notified and responded. They shot the whole scene, and afterwards I moved inside the police barriers. I was gloved and went over to the Dumpster. I looked inside, and it appeared to be 2/3 full of debris.

I saw that the lid to the tub was towards the back of the Dumpster. I kept looking inside to see if there was anything that would draw my attention and suggest we should remove all of the debris and go through it piece by piece. What I was thinking at the time was that all of the presented evidence was on top of the pile of debris. This was based on information given to us by Ms. Hanselman. The only thing that had been in the storage unit was the tub, which she had discarded on top of the debris. We didn't find out about Tyler until a week or so later. After the Dumpster was photographed both outside and inside, I checked the perimeter around it. Ms. Hanselman had stated that some fluid spilled onto her shoe and the ground as she was lifting it and putting it inside. I didn't see anything fresh, but the tub had been in the Dumpster for almost two days. The weather had been cloudy with spots of rain.

I then focused on the tub. It was photographed and, as I made my observations, I saw insect larvae inside it. Some body fluid was still there, and I noticed a circumferential demarcation line about 1″ from the bottom. I also noticed striation lines leading to the top of the tub. This meant the fluid had sloshed around and probably spilled over the top.

I decided not to swab the tub at this time. I figured this was something that could be done later at the crime lab. It would not have given us any immediate information, but we were taking it as evidence. I did collect larvae samples from the tub. I then checked the lid of the tub and noted the same insect larvae inside of it; samples of these were also taken.

I next tell the court about the Tommie Hilfiger canvas bag. I saw more insect larvae along the zippered part of the bag, and samples of these were collected. I opened it up and saw the child in the opened plastic garbage bag. I saw that the bag had been tied off at the end. I asked the crime scene tech to get some clean construction paper. They had a roll of it and brought over a section and laid it out on the ground. Before the remains of the child were taken out of the bag, OME was contacted and Dr. Erik Peters responded.

Once he arrived, he was briefed on the investigation. I then removed the child from the bag and placed it on the paper. The smell was horrible. Dr. Peters asked to have the legs stretched out, which I did. He took a measurement and said that the child was 32″ long, a female with reddish-brown hair. He said she was probably three years old. OME then took custody of the child, and the autopsy was scheduled for the next day.

I tell the court about the scene at the storage unit itself, #C19. I speak about not going inside the unit, but first having it photographed. I flashed a beam of light from a flashlight at floor level, looking for shoe prints. Prints were seen, and they were scaled and photographed. We then went in and noted a square pattern ring in the northeast corner.

The ring was formed from the body fluid that had collected inside the tub and eventually seeped through. I noticed a thin rope-type pull string attached to the light fixture. This was collected as evidence for possible DNA.

I believe the prosecution has covered all of the questions.

I'm then cross-examined by the defense.

Mr. O'Brien's overall goal is to make the investigation look flawed. He asks me why didn't I go inside the Dumpster and look for more evidence. I tell him it was because I believed that all of the evidence was on top of the debris.

He asks me why I didn't swab the area where the fluid dripped on Ms. Hanselman's shoe and ground. I tell him it was because we didn't need to at the time. He asks me why we didn't collect her shoes. I tell him we took photographs of her shoes and soles and from those we could match up the shoe patterns from the storage unit floor.

He asks if I know who removed the tub lid from the Dumpster. I tell him I think it was the CSS technician. He asks me if I searched the Dumpster. I tell him I didn't; I only looked inside. He asks if it's possible that Tyler's body could have been in there. I tell him it could have been. He asks me if I swabbed the tub. I tell him I did not.

At this point the judge wants to break for lunch, and the courtroom is adjourned.

I'm told by Sue that I won't be testifying any more today and that the cross-examination will resume later. She says that, because she's allowed to bring in Chris's drug history, she wants to present the video of Chris to the jurors, so the witness order has to be changed. When everyone returns from lunch, the jurors are advised that I'll be brought back at a later time.

Mike is brought in to testify and lay the foundation for the interrogation of Chris and how that all took place. Mike does a good job and covers all the details, answering the defense rebuttal questions.

The rest of the afternoon session consists of viewing the taped interrogation of Chris. The entire interview lasted five hours. The jurors and court hear about two hours of it. A lot of the video consisted of down time, where Chris was not being interviewed and was just being monitored.

Chris was his true self throughout the video; he was disgusting, rude, and manipulative. He was probably going through heroin withdrawal. He was, however, coherent and knew what he was doing and saying. I feel bad for Officer Gary Parrish, as he was the one watching Chris most of the time and had to deal with him. Chris was checked by the paramedics because of his physical complaints and was okay. Gary gave him coffee and snacks and took him to the bathroom several times.

Chris spit, blew snot on the wall, occasionally yelled, cussed, and banged the walls with his handcuffs. What was also very important about seeing the interrogation was the way he would try to manipulate the interviewer. In the short time I dealt with Chris, I knew him to be a vile, self-serving manipulator.

He initially spoke to Det. Mike Walker. Mike did a good job, considering. I later came in because Chris was acting up. Chris said he wanted to talk to me. I sat down and, after some questions, I called Mike back in, and we went forward with the interrogation. What the jurors and courtroom heard was Chris's explanation of what happened to his children.

The highlights of the interrogation began with Chris demanding to know why he was being held and questioned. Mike tried to get him to open up about his relationships with Jamie, Reina, and the kids. Chris answered some of the questions, but then wanted to speak to his father, Forrest Payne, and his sister. He was told that wasn't possible because his dad was on a flight going home, and his sister was not available.

Chris admitted to being addicted to heroin and said his preferred method of taking it was by smoking it. Mike eventually asked him about the kids. He said the last time he saw the kids was when they were living with Jamie, and that he'd had them for a weekend visit. He then wanted to say goodbye to Reina and his son, because he knew where this was going. After he was denied that, he began to cry. He said that he knew what this was all about.

He spoke about the kids and said that, when he got the kids, they were distraught and quit eating on him. He said he did everything he could to get them to eat, but they wouldn't. He said they soon began to eat their own feces. He was asked about what happened to the kids. He told Mike he knew what happened to them.

He was asked about Reina's involvement. He repeatedly said she wasn't involved. He said Reina was visiting her aunt when the kids died. Chris said he wasn't really working and was left alone to take care of the kids. He said he resorted to stealing food.

He said the kids wouldn't eat, and they just withered away. He said he didn't know what to do. CPS wouldn't help him, and he couldn't get food stamps. He said the kids wanted to be with their mother, but she was a meth addict, and he couldn't send them back because CPS wouldn't let him. He said he wanted to get help, but nobody would help him. He said they died about two months after he got them. He said they quit on him when they realized they weren't going back to their mother.

Chris said eventually the kids were beyond help and died within a week of each other. He said that Ariana died first, and then Tyler. He said he put them in a box—a "Rubbermaid" box. He thought they died sometime in July 2006. He said he knew he was in trouble, so he told Reina that the kids went back with Jamie.

He said all he wanted to do was be with Reina and his son. Chris proclaimed that Reina was the love of his life, and he would do anything for her and his son.

After Ariana died, he sat with her and prayed and prayed. He said he stayed with her for two days before moving her. He said that, when Tyler died, he kept him in the room for three days before moving him. He said he never got help for Tyler and knew he would die, too. Chris kept referring to Tyler and asked why only one set of bones was found in the tub. He seemed surprised that Tyler was not found in the tub with Ariana. He said he kept the kids in the outdoor storage closet for about one month before he moved them to the storage unit. He said the smell was getting bad. When Mike and I told him about Ariana's broken bones, he seemed surprised and said he never hit the kids.

Chris was also asked about the $19,000.00 in child support that he owed. He denied killing the kids over the child support. Chris still said he didn't kill the children, even though they died while they were under his care.

Chris did admit to soliciting Joshua to rent the storage unit for him. He said the kids were transported to the storage unit in the Plymouth. Chris also said that he thought he was a good father, but made some bad choices and should have got the kids some help.

These are some of the highlights of the videotaped interrogation. The courtroom is adjourned after listening to the interrogation for these two hours.

I find it hard to believe Chris could deny killing the kids. It's amazing that he would think they were responsible for their own deaths.

Day 4: Monday, March 2, 2009

The entire morning is spent listening to the rest of Chris's interrogation. Afterward, the court breaks for lunch. When everyone returns, the judge excuses everyone for the day. There are some legal issues that have to be taken care of behind closed doors with the attorneys. Reina is scheduled to testify for the next two days.

Today, the media made a big deal about the fact that I didn't swab the tub at the scene.

Day 5: Tuesday, March 3, 2009

The morning session begins by holding the jurors in the deliberation room. Mr. O'Brien makes a motion to exclude Reina's plea bargain from being heard in court, because he feels it's prejudicial to Chris. He says if the jurors hear the plea deal that Reina has accepted from the state, then they'll be biased and assume Chris is guilty, since they were together.

Sue objects to the motion and says it would not be prejudicial and should have no effect on the jury being biased towards Chris. After hearing both sides, Judge Fields denies the motion. The jurors are then called in.

Reina is brought in and takes the stand. The highlights of her interview begin with her talking about her relationship with Chris. She says they loved each other and eventually had a baby together. She then talks about Jamie and says she knew of her, but didn't speak to her very much. She knew that Jamie and Chris had the two children.

She says that, one day, Chris brought them home for a visit. He said Jamie was addicted to drugs, and he and Reina were going to take care of them. She says that, during the first couple of months with the kids, everything was normal, but it slowly changed. Chris started hitting them and isolating them in the bedroom and closet. She says Chris wouldn't feed the kids and left them to fend for themselves.

Reina says she really didn't care for the kids. She says that, with the kids there, she had a lot of extra responsibility. She blames her drug use for not properly caring for the kids. She says she should have done more for them. She says, now that she thinks about it, she can't believe she let this happen.

Reina says Chris would go out and sell drugs on a daily basis, and she would take care of the kids, including their son, Chris, Jr. She says Chris would be out until 11:00 at night, dealing drugs. She says she never got any support from him in this area and would get mad at him. She says Chris would get violent and beat her whenever she complained to him. She says this happened almost daily. Reina says Chris got her addicted to heroin, and they would smoke it together. She says that, in order to supplement their income, Chris would deal drugs and keep enough for them to use, too.

She says things got progressively worse. She says the kids were being isolated for long hours in the closet and were being fed very little. She says Chris would only give them a little bit of bread and water. She says she should have done more to help them, but was scared of Chris.

She says that some of his drug-dealing friends stayed with them for about one-and-a-half months. They would sleep in the living room, but were told to stay out of the bedroom. She says the kids were kept hidden in the bedroom and closet. Reina says Chris and she were in their bedroom, lying on the bed and getting high, while their friends were in the living room, sleeping.

She says at one point she had fallen asleep, and Chris woke her up and told her Ariana was not breathing. She says she was in shock and asked him what he meant. He brought Ariana out from the bedroom closet and laid her on the bed. He began CPR on her, but she was dead. He was freaking out and kept saying, "Oh, my God! Oh, my God! She's dead! She's dead! What are we gonna do?" She told him he had to keep quiet so no one in the next room would hear what was going on. She says he told her to get little Chris ready. He then took Ariana and put her back in the closet.

Reina says she remembers standing in the doorway of the closet and seeing Tyler lying down with his eyes open. He never said a word. They then closed the closet door and pushed a dresser in front of it. Tyler was left in the closet with his dead sister. They couldn't deal with this and left the apartment. They drove down to the local Circle K. She says they were in shock and at the time didn't know what to do. They knew they had to get back to the apartment. Once they were back, they got high again.

She says that, the next morning, Chris was supposed to go work the streets and sling heroin. She told Chris she didn't want to be alone with Ariana in the closet. He told Reina he was going to stay home. He then told Debra he wasn't going out that day. She left with the other guys to sling heroin. After the others left, Chris wrapped Ariana in the plastic bag, put her in the designer bag, and placed her in the outdoor storage closet. Reina says she never saw him wrap Ariana in the bags.

Reina says that, about a month before Tyler died, Chris had taken his belt and hit Tyler across the forehead, opening up a gash. Tyler was never treated for the injury, and the wound turned green. She says after Ariana died, she never checked on Tyler or saw him again until two weeks later. She says that was when he died. She says the smell in the apartment was terrible.

On that day, she and Chris were in the car, getting ready to leave. Chris sent her back to the apartment to check on Tyler. She went back to the apartment and into the bedroom. She had to move the dresser that was blocking the door to get into the closet.

She looked at Tyler and saw he was dead. She put the dresser back and ran downstairs. She got in the car and was quiet for a moment. Chris asked her what was wrong. She told him Tyler was dead. His reaction was, "Oh, fuck this!" He then started the car and drove over to a friend's house, where they got high.

Reina says they left Tyler in the bedroom closet. After a week had gone by, they decided to move out and rented an apartment on North Stone. She says that, when they left, they never turned in the keys. After another week had gone by, she told Chris they had to do something with the kids. She says they argued about it and decided to go back and get them.

After that, they came up with the plan to put Tyler in the tub with Ariana, and then move them to a storage unit. They later found Josh and asked him to rent the unit for them. After a couple of weeks, they moved the children's bodies. She says they left the apartment on North Stone because her mother called her and told her the police came by, asking for them. She says they were on the run.

They moved to the Palm Court Inn and left everything behind. They stayed there until Chris's father rented them a room at the Lazy 8 Motel. She says that was where the police caught up to them. Reina says she and Chris were wondering what they were going to do with the bodies. She says that Chris came up with the idea of taking them to Mexico. She agreed with him, but they never did go there.

Reina says that Chris told her, if the police caught them, she was not to tell them anything. She says he told her to tell them she didn't know anything. He told her to tell the police he put a gun to her head to force her to help him take the kids to the storage unit.

These are the highlights of her testimony. The defense is now given the chance to question Reina.

Reina admits to being a liar during the investigation. She says she did lie to the police throughout most of the interviews. The defense confronts her on all of her inconsistencies. At the end of it all, she does say she told the truth about what she and Chris did to those kids and how they died. The courtroom is very subdued when Reina speaks about the children. It's amazing to me that, whenever I look at Chris during the testimony, he doesn't show any reaction or emotion to anything. He is stone-faced.

Day 6: Wednesday, March 4, 2009

I'm called back to the stand to finish testifying. Sue covers the rest of the investigation with me, laying down the legal foundation to move on with the prosecution. She asks me about the initial scene, and why I never swabbed the tub.

I finish covering the scene and tell her we didn't swab the tub at the time because I decided to have the lab technicians process it in a controlled environment at the lab itself. She asks me if there are times when the County Attorney's office would call the lab and make requests directly to them without advising me. I tell her it does happen, and that it happened with the tub.

George Genung lived next door to Chris and Reina when they were living at the Portofino Apartments. He testifies that he never saw any kids at their apartment other than their two-year-old son. He says that, after a while, the apartment smelled as if something had died there. He says the TV was always on and played very loud.

Ana Ontiveros is the assistant apartment manager. She gives the timelines when Chris and Reina moved in and when they left. She also speaks about the condition of the apartment and the terrible smell. She says they never did rent the apartment after Chris and Reina left because of the smell and the condition it was in. She says the maintenance crew did go in and try to clean it up. At the time, they only painted the walls. She says they went in several months after Chris and Reina moved out of the apartment.

The court allows the witness list to be changed and go out of order. The defense is allowed to present some of its case because of the expert witness schedule.

Dr. Janice Ophoven is a pediatric pathologist hired by the defense (at $250.00 per hour, not including travel expenses). She has been called in to refute Dr. Anderson's testimony. Dr. Ophoven states that she has thirty years of experience in pathology and forensic pathology and has focused her practice on child abuse and injuries.

Dr. Ophoven speaks about the different stages that bone goes through as it heals and its remodeling process. She says that broken bones will heal at different rates and that an anthropologist is not qualified to give a healing timeline on bones. She says the only claim he can make about the bones is that it's an "old injury."

She claims the injuries to Ariana are from compression and believes she was either stomped on or something heavy was placed on top of her with her body on a hard surface. She also states that kids would not show or display any signs of pain with broken bones, which sounds ridiculous to me. She also states that a child would initially have pain with a shoulder injury, but not afterwards. She does agree that these are serious injuries.

She also speaks about the starvation process and says there would be depleted nutrients (scurvy) and that the skull would become thin, but still continue to grow. She does agree that, if there were a cut on the forehead, then it would probably bleed.

Sue questions Dr. Ophoven's qualifications and tears apart all of her theories and explanations. She is masterful in how she handles the doctor. Under cross-examination, Ophoven testifies that she was paid $12,000.00 to testify for the defense. In my opinion, Dr. Ophoven is there to confuse the jury. I feel she didn't hold up well during Sue's cross-examination, and I feel the jury isn't buying into her testimony.

Day 7: Thursday, March 5, 2009

Sue and Jack O'Brien finish with Dr. Ophoven.

Debbie Barbone, Christopher's stepsister, is called to the stand and testifies that she went to the jail on several occasions to visit him. She tells us about conversations she had with Chris. Sue then plays the video-recorded conversations. Chris again was no help to himself. He displayed how resentful he was and how he tried to manipulate Debbie and his family. He spoke of the kids, but was careful about what he would say.

This takes up most of the day.

Day 8: Friday, March 6, 2009

TPD Crime Scene Specialist Bill Greener is called to testify. He explains how he was notified to respond to the crime scene at the Portofino Apartments, how that scene was processed, and how the evidence was collected. He also explains the concept of Luminol and how it was used at the scene.

Bunkye handles the questioning of the DNA experts. She knows what they're talking about and has them explain DNA and its process in layman's terms.

Next to testify is Amy Smuts from Texas Laboratory Technologies. She explains how I called her and advised her of the investigation. She says she works for a grant-funded laboratory that conducts DNA tests in homicides for law enforcement and does charge them for their services. She advised me of the bones that were needed from the remains found at the scene, along with a DNA swab from the potential parents.

She says she received from Nora Rankin the items she asked for and processed them. She says the results concluded that DNA samples from the parents (Chris and Jamie) and the child remains were a match. Tests also revealed that the blood found on the carpet taken from inside the closet at the Portofino apartment was a DNA match for Tyler, Chris, and Jamie. A test that was done with another section of carpeting and a swab from the plywood floor from the apartment's outdoor storage closet revealed profiles that included both Tyler and Ariana.

The courtroom is adjourned for the weekend.

Day 9: Monday, March 9, 2009

Debra Reyes is called in to testify. She is wearing the Pima County Jail orange jump suit and is awaiting sentencing for her drug conviction. She confirms her relationship with Chris and verifies that he was one of her drug dealers. She verifies that she spent time at his Portofino apartment with three other dealers. She confirms that they were all selling heroin on a daily basis, and that they would be gone all day and most of the evening.

She states she respected Chris and Reina's privacy and never bothered them when they were in their bedroom. She says she never saw the two children, only little Chris. She says she thought she did hear a child's voice coming through the wall between the bathroom and the bedroom closet. She wasn't sure and didn't say or ask anything.

After lunch, TPD DNA expert Nora Rankin testifies. She explains the DNA process that TPD is able to do. She explains how other labs are sometimes called to conduct further tests. She explains how she came up with Tyler and Ariana's profile, and how she sent that information to the outside lab. She also testifies to sending the requested bones from Ariana's remains to the Texas Lab, maintaining the chain of custody.

Dr. Erik Peters from the Office of the Medical Examiner testifies. He speaks about his finding at the initial crime scene. He describes the autopsy he performed on Ariana and goes into detail as to why he was limited in what he was able to do. He says he consulted with Dr. Anderson, who then conducted the examination on Ariana's remains.

Day 10: Tuesday, March 10, 2009

Carolina Calderon testifies that she saw the children alive sometime between June-August 2006. She had gone over to visit her friend, Reina, and saw Tyler sitting on the couch. He had a bruise on his cheek and, when she asked who had hit him, he said his daddy hit him. She reported the incident to the child abuse hotline, but didn't give them the apartment number. She was probably the last person to see either of the kids alive.

Mirna Gonzales, Reina's aunt, is called to testify. She states that she used to be real close to Reina before she got into drugs. She says that, around February, before they were arrested, Reina came over asking her to notarize a document in case something happened to her and Chris. Mirna asked her about the kids, because they were not with her. Reina said they were with their dad. She says Reina was always asking her for money.

Mirna speaks about the night Chris was arrested. When it came out in the news, Reina came over and stayed for the night. Mirna asked her about the kids. Reina denied he had killed the kids. Mirna asked her where Tyler was. She said Chris was worried about them because he left them together. Mirna says Reina asked her about what she had said to the police. Mirna told her she'd told the police everything. After that, Reina shut down and didn't talk about it anymore. Mirna thought something was wrong with Reina because she kept twitching. The next morning, she called other family members, and they came over to pick her up. Mirna says she didn't see or hear from Reina after that.

Day 12: Wednesday, March 11, 2009

Forrest Payne, Chris's father, is very hostile with the prosecution. His wife, Patricia Payne, and he are not very cooperative with the state. They felt from the beginning that Reina was the one who murdered these kids, and that Chris was the scapegoat. They certainly were surprised when they found out the state was seeking the death penalty against Chris.

I can only imagine their pain. It has to be the worst nightmare anyone could possibly endure. Although I really couldn't care less about Chris or Reina, it's the family collateral damage that is devastating. I can't imagine losing two grandkids at the hands of their own father. It would be almost unbearable.

Forrest speaks about his visits every year. He's a member of the Tucson Rodeo Committee, and every February he comes down for two weeks for the rodeo. He speaks about his recent visit and how he called Chris, asking to see him and the grandkids. He says that Chris, Reina, and little Chris were staying at the Palm Court Inn.

Chris asked him for money and, as usual, Forrest gave him what he needed. When he asked about Tyler and Ariana, Chris told him they were visiting some friends.

Forrest testifies that he rented them a room at the Lazy 8 Motel and didn't know Chris had been arrested until he arrived home. Forrest tells the court that, around July or August, he came into town for a short visit and went over to the Portofino Apartments to visit Chris. When he arrived, he pounded on the door, but there was no answer. He thought someone was there because he heard the TV. He left when no one answered the door.

The next person to testify is Jean Nix. She was an employee at SKOR, a transportation service for the disabled. Chris worked there for about a month. She spoke about what a good employee he was when he was first hired, and then the transformation that occurred as he digressed and eventually was terminated. He came in late, missed a lot of time, and left whenever Reina would call and complain to him about the kids. She says Reina would call 3-4 times a day. It seemed to her that the calls started coming in more frequently, and Reina would be more panicked and angry each time. She says she could hear kids crying in the background.

Day 12: Thursday, March 12, 2009

Today the defense calls in their DNA expert, Kelly Fenesan. She's affiliated with Human Identification Technologies. She puts on a power point presentation about DNA. After the presentation, Ms. Fenesan is asked about the DNA collection and testing on this case. Her DNA findings and profiles are basically the same as the DNA findings and profiles from the TPD and Texas labs.

Day 13: Friday, March 13, 2009

This is an interesting day. CPS Supervisor Christy Tarpley and CPS caseworker Cindy Graupmann are called in to testify for the defense. Cindy is the first one to testify. She says she no longer works for CPS and is retired. Cindy says that in 2005 she began an investigation against Jamie Hallam because they'd received reports that she was neglecting Tyler and Ariana.

She says that during the investigation she suspected Jamie was using drugs. She says Jamie had sores on her face that were consistent with someone who was abusing drugs. She asked Jamie for a drug test. Jamie took the test three days later, and the test came back negative. Cindy says she made two surprise in-home visits, and each time the kids were healthy and dressed appropriately.

Cindy says she closed the case because there was not enough evidence to move on. Cindy believes that Jamie was on drugs and neglecting her kids, but she just didn't have the evidence. Cindy says that, even though the drug test came back negative, she considered it a positive test because Jamie waited three days to take the test.

Cindy says she became involved with Jamie again on March 1, 2006, when she told Jamie the investigation against her was closed. Jamie had even signed a document verifying the case against her was closed. She says that on March 9, 2006, she and her supervisor, Christy Tarpley, received a call from TPD advising them that Jamie was trying to pick up her children from their father, Chris Payne. Jamie apparently had court paperwork verifying that she had legal custody. The officers were told to leave the kids with Chris.

Cindy says she had called and told Jamie earlier that day that the case against her was still open, but there was no evidence of that in the case notes. Sue catches Cindy in a contradiction, and it doesn't look good. Sue shows how incompetent Cindy was as a CPS caseworker.

The defense tries to say that CPS was also out conducting domestic violence investigations to see if it was possible that one of Jamie's boyfriends had hurt Ariana and caused the injuries to her before Chris took the kids. No evidence was ever linked to prove that theory.

Christy Tarpley then testifies. She comes across as even more hostile than Cindy. She says she did receive a call from the officers on March 9, 2006. However, she says the officers told her that Chris had signed documentation showing he now had legal custody of the kids. Christy says she was not familiar with the case because she'd been assigned as supervisor for the day.

She says she didn't take the time to read the case notes in order to be familiar with the case and make the right decision. She also says she never told the police to leave the kids with Chris.

Christy came across to me as a cold-hearted person who didn't care about what she was doing and never protected the kids the way she should have. I should mention here that I've worked with CPS for eleven years, and these two do not accurately represent the CPS caseworkers, who do a wonderful job.

This case now comes to a close. There were other witnesses that testified. I left them out to protect their identities because of the relationship they have with little Chris. What also needs to be mentioned is that, during the court proceedings, there were consistent objections, sidebars, and closed meetings in the judge's chambers. All of this is very important in staying within the law and seeing that the trial is what it should be—fair and just.

What is important is the fact that the attorneys on both sides fought the best they could for both the victims and the accused. I have the utmost respect for Prosecutors Sue Easer and Bunkye Chi, Defense Attorneys Jack O'Brien and Rebecca McLean, and Judge Richard Fields. He controlled his court in a high profile trial; he was also fair and impartial. The closing statements will be made on Monday.

The Closing Statements

. . . .

Day 14: Monday, March 16, 2009

Sue begins with the prosecution's closing statements [the following taken from actual trial transcripts]:

SUE EAZER: Thank you.

The final weeks of their young lives were spent in a five-by-six, hot, dark closet, terrified, battered and broken, and starving to death. Their final resting place was a 25-gallon Tupperware tub.

Ladies and gentlemen, I want to begin by thanking each of you for the tremendous sacrifice you have made to spend the last four weeks here with us, and listening to the evidence in the case which has been unquestionably difficult at times. On behalf of the State, I thank you for your time and avid attention, and the devotion you've given on this case.

In a short while you will be instructed on the law in this case. And after closing arguments, the case will be given to you to decide. Before you begin your deliberations, I want to begin my closing by talking to you about the law that applies to the charges in this case.

Then I want to talk to you a little bit about the facts and the evidence which I submit to you has been proven, not beyond a reasonable doubt, but beyond any doubt, that the defendant has committed each and every one of the crimes charged in the Indictment.

The State has charged the defendant, Christopher Payne, with counts, two counts of first degree murder, two counts of child abuse, and two counts of concealing a dead body.

I want to talk to you about the elements of the offenses first, and what the State is required to prove, and then I'm going to talk to you about what evidence supports each and every one of those elements.

I'll start by talking to you first about first-degree murder. The crime of first-degree murder can be committed in two ways. And you were told in general instructions at the beginning of the case, but that seems like a very, very long time ago, so I want to go back over it with you a little bit now.

First degree murder in Arizona can be committed in two different ways. First, is premeditated murder. And I want to talk to you about what Arizona defines premeditated as, because oftentimes when we think about premeditated, we think there has to be a plan in advance, and a lengthy period of time and preparation.

But actually, in Arizona, premeditation means that the defendant intended to kill another human being, or knew he would kill another human being, and after forming that intent or knowledge, reflected on that decision before killing. It is that reflection that, regardless of length of time, that makes it first degree murder. So, doesn't have to be minutes, hours, days, you have to find actual reflection.

In order to prove first degree murder the State must prove that the defendant caused the death of another person, and the defendant knew or intended that he would cause the death of another person, and that he premeditated the death. Again, that he reflected upon it before he acted.

The second type of first degree murder is felony murder. And the Judge will instruct you that on felony murder the State has to show, I'm just going to go ahead and read you the statute that the Judge will instruct you on. Just one moment here.

That the defendant commits an underlying felony, and during the course of and in furtherance of that felony, either the defendant, or another person, causes the death of the children in this matter, the alleged victims in this matter.

In this case, obviously, the underlying felony is the child abuse, for failing to get medical attention for these children. And so, you have to find, number one, that the defendant either committed or was an accomplice to the commission of the underlying felony of child abuse. And that during the course of committing that crime, caused — he or another person caused the death of Ariana and Tyler Payne.

So, then we have to look at our child abuse statutes. Now there's two counts of child abuse in this case. The first count has to do with the broken bones that you heard that Ariana suffered before her death, the 12 broken ribs and the broken shoulder.

The second count of child abuse involves not getting medical treatment for these children. And the Judge will instruct you that the crime of intentional or knowing child abuse use [sic] requires proof that, under circumstance likely to produce death or serious physical injury, the defendant did one of three acts. Intentionally or knowingly caused physical injury; having the care or custody of the child placed that — intentionally, knowingly, caused or permitted the health of the child to be endangered, injured, I'm sorry injured; or the third way is placing the child in a situation where their person or health was endangered, again, having care or custody of the child.

Now, the first part of the child abuse statute, under circumstances likely to produce death or serious physical injury, I submit to you has, is automatically proven in this case because clearly it did result in death of these two children.

And further going to talk to you a little bit about the evidence and how it shows the [sic] Christopher Payne didn't commit child abuse just one way, but he committed it in all three fashions. All you have to find is one. But I will submit to you that it was committed in all three fashions in this case.

He knowingly caused injury to these children, to Ariana, by breaking her bones; he knowingly caused injury to these children, to Ariana and Tyler, by starving them to death, and not getting them medical attention, not doing anything to try and save their lives; and, finally, he placed them in a situation, clearly in a situation where their health or person was endangered by starving them to death, by leaving them in that closet to die.

The Judge will tell [sic] that with respect to both first degree murder and child abuse, there's two ways you can commit first degree murder, felony or premeditated. All 12 of you — well, the 12 of you who will be remaining as the final panel, all 12 of you don't have to agree on whether it was first degree murder, or felony murder, or both. You just have to find that the defendant committed it in one of the two ways. Doesn't have to be unanimity as to which way it was committed.

Although, I submit to you, by the time this case is given to you and you begin your deliberations, you will see that the defendant, in fact, committed first degree murder in both of the manners in which it can be, in which it has been alleged and which it can be committed.

Likewise, with child abuse, you've got the three different ways it can be committed. And again, you don't have to be unanimous in your decision as to how the child abuse was, in fact, committed. You each just have to find that one of the ways, in fact, occurred in this case.

And once again, ladies and gentlemen, I submit to you by the time you go back in that jury room, after you've heard closing arguments, been instructed on the law, and look back upon the evidence presented in this case, you will find, again, that the defendant committed each of the three ways.

Now, I want to talk a little about the evidence in this case. And specifically, the Judge is going to instruct you, likewise, on evidence. And I think you had this instruction as well in your preliminary instructions. Evidence can be direct or circumstantial. Direct evidence is evidence of an eyewitness testimony, for example. And circumstantial evidence is proof of a fact or facts from which you can infer another fact.

So, I think the example on, most common example is that — might even be one that is given in your instructions, is if I come into the courtroom and I'm soaking wet and I tell you, hey, I just came in from outside and it's raining outside, that would be direct evidence. I've just come in. I've been outside. I tell you it's raining outside.

Circumstantial evidence would be, I come in. I don't say a word to you, but I'm wearing my raincoat and I'm dripping wet. My hair is soaking wet. And from that you can infer I just came in from outside, and it's probably raining outside.

In this case there's abundance of both types of evidence, direct and circumstantial evidence. An example would be, direct evidence would be, let's say, Carolina Calderon, who came in and testified that on one of the occasions when she was visiting Reina Gonzales, she saw Tyler with bruises all over his face. Eyewitness testimony, what she actually observed.

Circumstantial evidence, likewise, in this case, there's a tremendous amount of it. An example would be when people came to the home during the months of June, July, and August, and the children were not there. Or when the defendant and Reina would go out to people, you know, to other people's houses, and would not have Ariana and Tyler. Circumstantial evidence that on those occasions those children were, in fact, in the closet, just as Reina Gonzales testified.

Now, a large percentage, a large majority of the evidence that you're going to consider in this case obviously came from the witness stand, the witnesses who testified at trial. You also are going to have exhibits and photographs, and a number of different things that were admitted during the course of the trial. But in large part, you're going to have to rely upon witness testimony.

And the Judge is going to instruct you on witness testimony. Specifically, the Judge is going to tell you that you all have to decide the believability of witnesses. In doing so, take into account such things as their ability and opportunity to observe, their memory and manner while testifying, any motive or prejudice they might have, and inconsistent statements that they've made.

And the last part of this instruction, I believe, is the most important part. You are to consider each witness' testimony in light of all the evidence in the case.

And what this means, ladies and gentlemen, is you look at the witnesses' testimony, and when you put it together with all the other evidence that you're going to be considering in this case, it's like each piece of evidence is a piece to the puzzle. And in the end, it all should fit pretty nicely.

Now, of course, there's never going to be a perfect fit because witnesses' memories wane after years. There might be things that someone doesn't remember, or doesn't recall precisely, but, for the most part, it all should fit. Witnesses' testimony should be consistent, time lines should fit within the time line, and you need to consider all of the evidence as a whole. And that's really, really important.

So if you've got one witness who's saying something that totally is contradictory to everything else that every other witness in the courtroom talked about, or if you have evidence that's totally contradictory, that should be a red flag to you that there's [sic] problem with that piece of evidence.

I'm going to talk about that a little bit more when we talk about the defendant's statement to law enforcement that he made on March 1st of 2007.

All right. So, when we're looking at the witnesses' testimony, ladies and gentlemen, I want you to keep in mind a couple of things. Number one, as you saw throughout the course of this trial, obviously, people who are heroin addicts, are using drugs, don't have the best recall for dates and times.

But there's other ways that we can gather our dates and times and form a time line of what happened in this case, when it happened, and so forth. And that's because we had some very specific dates. As you noticed throughout the course of the trial, there would be times when I went to the board. And I would write down a certain date, or we'd look at the lease agreement, or defendant's employment records, and so forth, because those are certain dates from which we can now have at least a foundation for a time line. So I want to talk to you a little bit about that time line and what it tells us in this case.

Now, what we know, what we do know and what we can say with assurance is, that during the months of October through December of 2005, the children, Ariana and Tyler, were living with their mother and their grandfather, Richard Barcelow. We know this through not only the testimony of Jamie Hallam, but through Richard Barcelow, through Forrest Payne, who visited the children, as you'll recall, at their grandfather's house around Christmas time of 2005. And we know it from Cindy Graupman, the CPS worker who you heard from late last week. She went — who went to the home on two different occasions and saw the children.

What we do know, that during — is during this time the children were happy, healthy, and they [sic] well-cared for. And again, we know that from Jamie, who testified about her children and the last months of their young lives. We know that from Richard Barcelow, who said his grandchildren were healthy, ate well, were happy, playful, they interacted well. They loved each other. Never had a problem feeding them. They, in fact, he said they cost a lot of money to feed because they liked to eat.

We know it from Forrest Payne, again, who said the children looked fine. They were shiny and clean and they looked fine to him when he visited with the children at their grandfather's house in December of 2005. And we know it from the reluctant Cindy

Graupman, who had to reluctantly admit that the children were clean, they were with [sic] well-dressed, they were well-behaved, that she saw absolutely no sign of neglect or abuse.

And remember one thing that's important about Cindy Graupman, I mean, obviously, she had her own agenda going on here, but when she went to visit those kids, as you'll recall, on both occasions it was a surprise visit. Jamie didn't have time to, like, know that CPS was coming, to clean the kids up, make them, you know, look good for CPS. They were surprise visits. And both visits found those children healthy, happy, well-cared for, with no signs of neglect.

What we also know from the testimony during this trial is that in mid-January of 2006, the children then went to the defendant and Reina. Jamie Hallam, as you'll recall, said that when — she recalls very, very clearly the date that she last dropped those children off with the defendant, January 20th, 2006.

Defendant likewise makes statements to CPS, that he had the children when he speaks to CPS in February. That he'd had the children for a few weeks and, therefore, putting us into January. Likewise, Reina, although she had problems with her time line and remembering dates and so forth, she remembers the children were with them for a period of time after Christmas. They had a visit at Christmas time. They were with them after Christmas. And they were with them before the Super Bowl which I now know happens in February, not January. So we know that the defendant now has those children in his care and in his custody.

We know, in February of 2006, that the children are still in the defendant and Reina's care and custody, and that they are healthy, and that there are no signs of trauma. This is really significant, it's going to become real important for a lot of reasons I'm going to talk to you about further in a moment.

But how do we know that during February of 2006 these children were healthy and have no signs of trauma or neglect? Forrest Payne. He sees the children both at the rodeo and over at the grandmother's house, his mother's, or Pat's mother's house for some type of a family event.

Says those kids were well-dressed. They had expensive shoes on. And to use his words, they were healthy as bears. No signs of neglect. No signs of malnourishment. They were healthy as bears.

We know from Debbie Barbone who also saw them at the rodeo that the kids were healthy. Again, no signs of neglect.

And, finally, we know from Carolina Calderon that the children were healthy, playful, and doing just fine, thriving just fine in February of 2006 when she went over to the defendant's home, apartment, for the Super Bowl party.

We know that in March through mid-April 2006, again, that the children are healthy, and there's no signs of trauma, there's no signs of neglect. We know this from Donna Atkinson who saw the children somewhere around Easter time.

And we know Easter, I think, was on the 17th, I believe, of April. So Donna Atkinson sees them somewhere either late March or early April. Says that they were dressed nicely. She remembers Ariana was in a little summer dress and looked really cute. That there was no sign of abuse, no sign of trauma. And, clearly, the children were not withering away and not eating at this time.

We also know this from Forrest Payne who, again, sees the children during that same time frame, again, at the grandmother's house. We know this from Officer Nutt and Officer Gomez who go to the defendant's apartment on the 9th of March of 2006 and see the children. And they're fine. They're healthy. No signs of trauma. No signs of neglect. They had no concerns about leaving those children with the defendant and Reina Gonzales in early March of 2006.

Now, then we get to April 6th, 2006. Again, here's another date for which we can now again build our foundation for when certain things happened in this case.

Because April 6th, we know, is the date that the defendant got fired from SKOR. And this is going to be a really important marker, obviously, in our time line and what ultimately happened to Ariana and Tyler Payne.

We know that after the defendant gets fired from SKOR, according to both Reina, and according to Debbie Reyes, he doesn't work for a while. He doesn't immediately start working with Debbie Reyes. Reina said he stayed home for a month or two.

And he's not working, he's not going anywhere. He's pretty much, according to Reina, they're just staying home and getting stoned every day, getting high on heroin every day, for at least a month. And Reina said maybe as much as two months.

Debbie Reyes, who, as you will recall, is certainly — has no love lost for Reina in this case, never saw any of the [sic] Reina's statements, never talked to Reina. Nonetheless corroborates what Reina says, because she recalled that it was after the defendant got fired from SKOR, but not immediately after he got fired from SKOR. She said it was a few weeks.

First he was just her client, you'll recall. He was just buying heroin from her. He didn't immediately start working with her. She said it was at least [sic] few weeks after he got fired from SKOR before he actually began working with her.

Well, now we have our turning point. Now we start to see thing [sic] happening with these children. April 15th, you'll recall the testimony of Terry White. And again, when you're looking at witnesses and their credibility, ladies and gentlemen, one of the things that's going to be really important to keep in mind is Terry White clearly didn't want to come in this courtroom and testify against her nephew. She didn't want, you know, you saw her mouth, I love you, to him as she walked in the courtroom, as she walked out. She had absolutely — has no motive to lie about what she saw or what she said when this investigation first began.

But what does Terry White tell us? She was reluctant. She didn't want to say bad things, and come in here and hurt her nephew. But, but what she said was, is Ariana was not well. And remember, she tried to kind of, you know, soften it around the edges, but that's why I read to her, and read to you, the statements that she gave to the police at that time. And you get to consider those statements just as much as you get to consider her testimony. But she was worried about that little girl on that date.

She said she was scrawny, real scrawny. Real skinny. Her hair was a mess. She looked very unhappy. She said the house was a mess. There was dirty dishes everywhere. There was trash everywhere. The house was a mess.

And she said the defendant was yelling at the children and that he had no patience for those kids. Okay. So this is clearly important because, you know, what became very, very clear from the moment this case started is, the defendant wants to say all this bad stuff happened to his kids while he was off working all day, and Reina was home. And, therefore, Reina must have done it. And we're going to talk a lot about that in just a moment.

But clearly here you have the defendant home. The defendant with the kids. Reina is in the other room sleeping. And his own relative was very concerned about what she saw that day.

So through April to mid May of 2006, you have defendant not [sic] home, not working. But what we also have is now we start having evidence that the children were being kept in the closet on occasion. And you'll recall Reina Gonzales' testimony. It didn't, you know, it started out, you know, just here and there. When they would be bad, they would be put in the closet. Or when Reina and Christopher had to go somewhere, they would be put in the closet. Then it gradually got to more and more and more hours, and more times that they would be put in the closet until, eventually, they were in that closet 24 hours a day, seven days a week, for close to the last two months of their lives.

Well, you know, and defense is going to have lots to say, I'm sure, about Reina, as he did when she took the stand, about her credibility and whether she's lying to you. But let's talk about where, where's Reina's testimony corroborated?

And I'm going to stop right here on Reina and talk to you for a moment about her. Because, you know, folks, I will tell you right now, as we did in opening, no one is going to say Reina was a great mother. No one is going to say Reina was a good mother. I'm not here to tell you Reina was even a good person. What she did was awful. Horrendous. Horrific.

But she got up on that stand, and she told you she could have helped them, and she didn't. She could have snuck them food, and she didn't. She could have called the police, and she didn't.

She could have made up a story that she wasn't there, or that she didn't know. But she got up there and she told you things that weren't in the defendant's statement. You recall when Mr. O'Brien was questioning her, he said, you got a chance to read the defendant's statement and all the disclosure in this case. And then you come in here, and you give this statement to the State and you get a dandy plea offer from the State as a result of it.

Well, think about it, folks. She read the defendant's statement, which you heard in its entirety. He didn't say anything about locking those kids in the closet. He said those kids starved themselves to death. That they quit eating on him, and he didn't know what to do. And he was distraught.

So if Reina, after reading the defendant's statement, trying to come up with what she needs to say to get a deal, why didn't she stick with that story? The kids stopped eating. We didn't know what to do. They got too skinny. We knew we couldn't, if we took them to get help then we'd get in trouble with the police and lose our son Christopher. Why did she come up with something so much worse?

Why did she come up with something that made her into an even more horrible person by admitting she was home alone with those kids and she could have done something, but she didn't. Why did she talk about seeing the gash in Tyler's head, and knowing that he's laying there in the closet, suffering as it festers and gets infected to the point of turning green?

Think about that when you're thinking about whether or not Reina Gonzales was believable, and whether her testimony was believable, and whether she is a reliable witness, despite the fact that she was a heroin addict, despite the fact she did nothing to help those kids.

So Reina tells us that he's home, not working, and what's happening during this month of April and May? They're using more and more heroin every day. They're sitting home and they're getting high all day long. And that's when Reina tells us things start getting bad. That's when everything takes a turn. She says everything was okay up until the time he lost his job from SKOR, at SKOR, and then things started getting bad.

Again, is there corroboration for what she says? Absolutely. Up until this time, Reina is home taking care of the kids. But they're healthy, they appear well-cared for, there's no signs of neglect. But after this time now, we start seeing things happening with those children. And again, when you see corroboration for witnesses' testimony, obviously, ladies and gentlemen, I would argue to you that's a pretty good indicator that the witness is telling the truth.

So Reina says everything starts going downhill after he loses his job. And sure enough, we know not only from Terry White's testimony, but we have the first indication that those children are being kept in the closet in early May. And you'll recall Donna Atkinson's testimony, that was right around little Chris' birthday. It was either the weekend of or very close in time to little Chris' birthday.

And Reina and the defendant and little Chris Junior show up at her house. And they said they'd just come from the park where they were having a little birthday party for little Chris Junior. And Donna asked, well, where are Ariana and Tyler? And the response was, they wanted to stay home and play with the neighbor kids.

Folks, you all know those — Ariana and Tyler did not stay home and play with any neighbor kids at the Portofino Apartments. Those kids were in the closet.

So we know that at least by May, consistent with Reina's testimony. These kids are now being put in the closet when they have to go out, or when, you know, they're bad, and so forth.

We know mid-May to June the defendant begins working with Debbie Reyes. We knows this from Reina's testimony again. And defendant acknowledges that he's, in his statement to the police, that he's out selling drugs. So mid-May to June, now he's working with Debbie Reyes. And as you'll recall from Debbie Reyes' testimony, he's not working with her full-time right off the bat. He's working some days with her, and doesn't become full-time until after he bails her out of jail, was her testimony. When we got up there and actually gave her some dates that she could think about and put in perspective for going back in time, he begins, he's just working with her just part-time.

Now, we have another identifiable date that is, well, again, mid-June. We know the children are in the closet again because Forrest Payne testified that he went to the house. And you'll recall it was sometime in mid-June, he goes to the house. He's banging on the door. Nobody answers. And again, where's our corroboration for Reina Gonzales? Reina tells us that there was an occasion when Forrest came over to the house, and the defendant tells her and Chris, little Chris, to be quiet. Because they don't want to answer the door.

And sure enough, Forrest tells the police back in March when this all begins, when the investigation begins, there was time in January, I mean in June, that he went over there a couple of different times, bangs on the door, and nobody answers. But he thinks it's odd because the car is out in the parking lot.

Well, why didn't they answer the door, folks? And why did Chris, why did the defendant only have to tell Reina and little Chris to be quiet? Because the other kids were in [sic] closet.

June 22nd, took paperwork, Debbie Reyes, as to when defendant bailed her out of jail. And now, shortly after he bails her out of jail, he begins working full-time with her, you'll recall. And a

short time after that shes moves in with him. And she and her associates move in with him.

And we know by the time Debbie Reyes and her associates
start staying with the defendant, those children are in the closet 24
hours a day, seven days a week. Because no one ever sees them.

But Debbie tells us things that are indicative of, in fact, they
were in the closet. And at least for a period of time while she was
living there, those kids are still alive. She hears the noises from the
closet, you know, through the bathroom wall. And remember the
diagram of the apartment. The shower wall is the one that abuts
to the closet where those children are. She's hears noise. She hears
cries that didn't sound like little Christopher.

And I would submit to you, ladies and gentlemen, that Debbie
Reyes was in the living room when Chris found, the defendant
found little Ariana dead and brought her out and laid her on the
bed. Remember she said there was a commotion? She talked about
there was a commotion in the bedroom. And she heard all sorts
of noises. And she knocks on the door to see what's wrong. That, I
would submit to you, is the occasion, what she was hearing when
he pulled Ariana from the closet and he freaked out.

And then, we know he puts his deceased daughter's lifeless,
cold body back into the closet with his son who is still alive. And
Chris Payne and Reina go out and get high.

This, ladies and gentlemen, I submit to you, are some of the
dates and times that you can rely upon in deciding what happened
in this case.

So now let's talk about some of the other evidence in this case.
You have, Reina Gonzales tells us that while she does not see Chris
do, the defendant do anything that she perceived could have broken the ribs and so forth, or broken little Ariana's ribs and bones,
that she doesn't see when he disciplines the children. He oftentimes would go to the bedroom, close the door, and she would
hear crying, but she didn't actually see what he did.

She saw him on a couple of occasions spanking his kids with a belt or his hand. And she saw one occasion where he hit Christopher — or he hit Tyler with a belt, and the belt buckle hits him in the head, and causes the gash in his head which later becomes very, very infected. So she sees, she sees some of the discipline, but doesn't see all of them.

Likewise, folks, you heard from a number of witnesses that Chris Payne, the defendant, was the one who was in charge of disciplining those kids. He was the main disciplinarian in the house. And I would submit to you, ladies and gentlemen, that, circumstantially, what we can tell from our time line, is at the point when the children no longer come out of the closet, I would submit to you, or they're leaving them in the closet because they're going someplace and can't take those kids, the reason they can't take them is because of the abuse. Is because there had to be signs when Ariana's little ribs were broken, and her shoulder's broken.

That's the time, ladies and gentlemen, I would submit to you, that closet became Ariana and Tyler's permanent place. Because they could no longer have the kids out and about. And that, ladies and gentlemen, is why Reina Gonzales didn't notice signs of Ariana having broken ribs, because she never went in the closet again. Couple of times when she looked in she didn't touch the children. She looked in the closet. She sees them huddled and lying on the floor. We know from statements of the defendant himself, which I'm going to talk to you about in just a moment, that these children, over a period of time, gradually starved to death.

Now, the one dispute being is he said they starved themself [sic] to death. I would submit to you, ladies and gentlemen, these children didn't starve themselves to death, the defendant starved them.

So what else can we tell from our time line? Well, I'll tell you what, we talked a little bit about what the evidence is in this case, I want to talk to you about what is not, what is not evidence in this case.

From the beginning of this case, you heard a whole lot about what an awful mother Jamie Hallam was. About how she was [sic] meth addict. About how she neglected her kids. And how they were subjected to domestic violence in the home.

You heard inferences that these children were already injured before they came to stay with Christopher Payne and Reina Gonzales.

Well, the evidence certainly doesn't bear that out, ladies and gentlemen. In fact, the evidence is very clear those children were not injured prior to the time they came to live with the defendant and Reina Gonzales.

And, you know, Dr. Ophoven, she tried real hard to stretch the amount of time that those bones could have broken. But think about it, folks. Okay. You had Dr. Anderson who came in here and told you that it was weeks to months, they were weeks to months old. That you really can't definitively say when it was, but the very outer limits, he said eight months. And he even thought that would be stretching it, because there was still a great deal of callus formation.

And you wouldn't — you would expect, if it was over eight months, that you would have seen greater signs of healing. And, eventually, the ribs go back to their normal state, and you can hardly, you can't tell there's a fracture unless you look at the bone marrow.

So outside, eight months. Well, Dr. Ophoven tried really hard to stretch that. Well, could be a year. But in the end, what does Dr. Ophoven tell us? We paid her $12,000 to come in and tell us, I just don't know.

But we do, folks. Because, you know what? You don't have to be an expert. You don't have to be a physician to know that if your three-year-old child has 12 broken ribs, it is going to hurt. They're going to show some signs of being in pain. Especially if the broken ribs are not treated.

A child who's arm is literally, shoulder is literally broke, through and through-type break from a jerking motion, is going to show signs of pain, especially if the break is not treated.

So we know that from October to December, we don't have any evidence whatsoever, and October is really, even if you have Dr. Ophoven's time line of could be a year, that's putting us, you know, back in October through December. So we can stretch it back to when the kids were in Jamie Hallam's care.

So even if you wanted to push it past the eight months that Dr. Anderson talked to us about, there is nothing, no evidence that would support a finding that Ariana was injured during this time frame of October to December 2005. None whatsoever.

She is seen by lots of people. She is seen by CPS. And that child would have shown signs of suffering with 12 broken ribs and a broken shoulder.

What else in the evidence? Well, Jamie and how abusive she was. Well, again, you heard, Jamie admitted, yeah, that she had problems with drugs at different times in her life. She acknowledged that she didn't always do everything just perfect as a mom.

She loved those kids. You heard from her father, her mother, from Forrest Payne, the defendant's father, those kids weren't neglected in her care. You heard about domestic violence. You know, these kids were subjected to domestic violence. You heard no evidence, and there was no evidence that those children were ever abused by Jamie or any of her boyfriends that, you know, whose names were bandied about.

What else is not evidence? Well, that Reina Gonzales did this. Think about it, folks. You know, I mean, again, one of the most important things you're going to take when you go back in that jury room is your common sense. You know, think about it. Reina Gonzales did this.

Well, couple of things that should be, you know, you should be questioning in your mind. If Reina was beating these children, locking them in the closet, and was doing all this abuse, why is she calling the defendant several times a day and asking him to come home and take care of the kids? That just doesn't make sense.

You know, they argue on the one hand, she's calling, saying, you need to come home and take care of these kids. But if she's beating them, and if she's locking them in the closet, why is she calling him and telling him to come home and take care of his children?

Another thing you need to think about as far as this Reina Gonzales did this. You heard, you know, this man, for about five hours in the interview with police, and he blames everybody in the world for all of his problems, for all of his wrongs. It's everybody else's fault. The kids were in cahoots against me. The kids planned this. They wouldn't — they stopped eating. They started doing things that grossed me out.

He blamed his own children's death on his children. CPS wouldn't help me. Their mother was a bad mother. They came to me all messed up because Jamie messed them up.

I'll tell you one thing that is very, very clear from listening to defendant's statement, Christopher Payne didn't have any problem dropping the dime on somebody else and blaming somebody else for all his problems.

So if Reina had done these things, do you think he's really going to protect her at the risk of himself? This is from the statement, I will tell you, I will submit to you, this is one of the most selfish men around. He's not going to take the blame for Reina Gonzales.

And what does he say in his statement? Reina had nothing to do with it. He even tries to go so far as to say she wasn't there. I will submit to you, ladies and gentlemen, the reason why he's telling the detectives she wasn't even there, she doesn't know anything about it, he was hoping they wouldn't talk to her. He was hoping to keep her completely out of it.

You know, I'll submit to you the reason he wanted to keep her completely out of it from day one, is because he didn't want her to tell the police what he had done.

He didn't want her to tell the police that these children just didn't mysteriously starve to death. They were starved to death. He didn't want her to tell the police what she did tell the police eventually, and what she told you in this courtroom. That those kids were kept hostage in a closet for two months, and were not fed until they died.

Talk to you about the defendant's statements a little bit. Before I do, let me talk about one other thing that is not evidence in this case. Or there was no evidence of in this case. And that is, the defendant tried to get help from CPS. Throughout his statement, I tried to get help. I asked them for help. They wouldn't, you know, I tried to get food stamps. Not one single shred of evidence that he did that.

In fact, the CPS records support that, in February, when CPS went out to the defendant's house, they offered him assistance. They gave him numbers to call. They offered to take him down to the Salvation Army Food Bank so he could set up a monthly food box. He turned it down. And not one shred of evidence that he ever placed a call to CPS, DES, or any agency, AHCCCS, or Salvation Army, or any agency, to get those kids help, to get assistance with food. No evidence that he did what he could have done at any time and saved those children's lives.

When you're looking at whether or not this defendant committed child abuse, and whether he committed first degree murder, both premeditated and felony murder, one of the things that I'd say is some of the strongest evidence in this case is what the defendant himself tell [sic] us about their condition.

I could see their ribs, man. They just got so skinny. They looked like Ethiopians, man. It happened in my care, because I was f'ing — I was neglectful of the f'ing fact of making a phone call. The situation was too far gone. I failed to make the phone call because they were too far gone, man. The kids were just skin and bones.

When asked: Were you in control?

His reply was: Always.

How did Tyler die, was the question from the detective.

From malnourishment, man. They were so f'ing skinny, man. It took, like, about two months after they came, before they passed. She died of being too skinny. They got skinny, skinny, man. It would piss me off.

But here's what's really telling about why Christopher Payne didn't seek to get his kids medical care, why he didn't do anything that could have saved their lives, and what turns this from just felony murder into premeditated murder:

I was scared because they weren't eating. And it was pissing me off. And it was freaking me out because of how skinny they were getting. And didn't want anybody to know, because I might get in trouble. The state they were in, I didn't want to take them anywhere. They were acting bad and they were incontinent.

The detective says: You should have gotten those kids medical care.

I know I should have. That's the only thing I'm guilty. I knew that if I went and tried to get them help, I was already going to be in trouble, man.

At least five occasions, through Christopher Payne's statement, he said he couldn't take those kids to the doctor, didn't try to get them help, because he knew if he did he would get in trouble because they already were so far gone. And so what did he do? He sat back, and he let them die, to save himself.

He didn't have, you know, just a moment or two, or five minutes to reflect, as if someone, you know, picks up a gun and shoots someone. He didn't have just a moment or two. He had days. He had weeks. He had months. He sat back and he let those children slowly, painfully, starve to death.

That is child abuse. To knowingly cause injury to those children by starving them, by breaking Ariana's bones. He permitted them to suffer further injury.

The second way you can commit child abuse, by leaving them in that closet and failing to get them medical treatment, and starving them to death. And he placed their lives in imminent danger. Not just danger, but imminent danger, by failing to seek medical treatment for those children when they were starving to death.

During the course of committing child abuse, and in furtherance of committing child abuse, two children died. And that's felony murder. The fact that he reflected and had time to reflect, and sat back and let them die is premeditated murder of the worst kind.

Ladies and gentlemen, when you get done with your deliberations, the Judge is going to give you, when you begin your deliberations, the Judge is going to give you verdict forms. And on those verdict forms you're going to be asked to determine, on the first degree murder count, whether it was premeditated, or whether it was felony murder, or whether it was both. You're going to be asked to put down the number of you who find it to be premeditated, or felony, or both.

I am going to ask you, ladies and gentlemen, I am asking you, I'm imploring you, to put a checkmark and a number 12 beside premeditated murder. To put a checkmark and a number 12 beside felony murder. To put a checkmark and a number 12 beside both.

I'm asking you to hold this man accountable for what he did to three-year-old Ariana and four-year-old Tyler. First degree murder as sure as if he picked up a gun and shot them.

Thank you.

MR. O'BRIEN: Thank you, Judge.

Counsel for the State, please the Court, good afternoon, members of the jury. And as Ms. Eazer did, I would also like to thank you for the close attention and time that you've provided the Court, and Mr. Payne, and the State of Arizona, over the last month.

This is not an easy case. It hasn't been a pleasant case to listen to. It isn't going to be a pleasant case to decide. And you truly have the hardest job of any of us here in the courtroom, because you are the finders of the facts.

You will decide, to the best of your ability, given the information and evidence that the State has produced, what happened. What happened to Tyler, what happened to Ariana, during those months between January of 2006, and September, August, or September [sic] 2006.

Those children deserved better. There's no doubt about that. They deserved better from Christopher Payne. They deserved better from Reina Gonzales. They deserved better from Jamie Hallam. They deserved better from Child Protective Services. They deserved better from Tucson Police Department. They deserved better from the relatives who knew that children were there and for whatever reason weren't able to check on them, on both sides of the family.

So please understand that nothing that I say to you this afternoon is intended in any way, shape, or form, to diminish that those children deserved better and were failed by a perfect storm, as it were, of mistakes, neglect, inattention, and abuse. They deserved better.

I'm not going to stand here and tell you that the children killed themselves. I'm not going to tell you that they did this to themselves. I'm not going to try and even persuade you that they were in any [sic] responsible for what happened to them.

They were beautiful, innocent children. You've seen their photographs. They're beautiful children. You've seen the photographs that were taken of them when they were healthy, when they were together, when they were happy. And, sadly, you saw the photographs of Ariana after she had been dead for a period of months, when she was taken out of the storage closet. Not pleasant. Not something you want to remember.

But to a certain extent that photograph is not evidence of what happened during the months in question. The photograph, as ugly as it is, as gruesome as it is, as distressing as it is, is not evidence of what happened in the apartment at Portofino. It's evidence of what the condition of body was months, half year later. But it's not evidence of what happened in that apartment.

Now, in a case like this, I sometimes don't know where to start. We've all sat here and listened to the same evidence over the last three weeks, four weeks, and have different opinions. I expect that's why there are 12 of you here, or 16, will turn to 12, who will deliberate and decide this case. So that your consensus, your discussions, your opinions, all come to bear as a crucible of truth.

Each of you is entitled to an individual opinion in this case, to individually find the facts in this case, and to bring that opinion to the group as you discuss what happened.

State's counsel made reference to a lot of things, and I'll address as many as I can remember. But one of the things that struck me was her statement that this is like putting together a puzzle. And there's a part of me that doesn't disagree with that, though calling it a puzzle in a sense trivializes the tragedy that you're deciding now. But, what I submit to you is, there's a couple of rules about puzzle solving, putting together a puzzle.

And the first rule is that you can't take a piece of—a scissors, to the pieces of the puzzle, and cut them so that they fit. You have to use all of the pieces in the puzzle in order to say that you put the puzzle together. And really, what you have in this case, you might think of as a puzzle that might be this big.

And what the State has done, is they've snipped and they've cut the pieces, and they put them together. And if the puzzle was supposed to be three by three, they've shown you something that' s one by one and they said, look, that's all you need to look at. We've solved the puzzle.

How do you know this? You know this by the things that you've heard and things that you haven't heard. And I'll remind you of what the Judge has told you, and will tell you again, the evidence comes from this chair. The evidence isn't what I say. It's not what Ms. Eazer says. It's what the witnesses say. It's what they say completely. We don't pick and choose. We don't select the part of the testimony that fit [sic] our time line, and ignore the rest.

And one of the things that you're entitled to ask yourselves is, why is it that it appears that the standard for being on the time line during the period of time that matters, is being a heroin addict?

Why is it, for example, and this is but one example, why is it that you don't see the testimony of Ms. Calderon, who says that she was over at the apartment visiting a couple of times a week, over the course of the summer? And that the children were out. That she saw them.

That the last time she saw them was around her birthday. And she couldn't remember if it was before her birthday, or after her birthday, but it was around her birthday. She first said I think before. But that didn't quite fit with the time line. So further questioning from the State got her to, well, maybe it was before. I don't remember.

Well, that doesn't fit into this box that has Reina Gonzales, Debra Reyes, and part of Christopher Payne's story, with a little snippet of some other witnesses who came by and I'll address those as I go along.

But what's the significance of this? Well, the significance of this is that if Ms. Calderon is visiting throughout the summer, and is seeing the children, then the children aren't in the closet 24-76 [sic]. Because she saw the children.

Ms. Eazer reported to you that Ms. Calderon said that there were, I think her words were bruises, all over his face. You'll recall the testimony, many of you were taking good notes. I assume good notes. And you'll recall specifically what her testimony was about a bruise on one side of his face, not all over his face. But that's the overstatement that plays into the emotions of this case in order to secure the State's goal of having you say, oh, this must be first degree murder.

But, Ms. Calderon, who saw these children, did not see, for example, an open wound on Tyler's head that was infected and untreated and green.

Can't we ask if she had seen that? Don't you think she would have related that to us? Don't you think that would have been something that she would have noticed in her twice weekly visits with Ms. Gonzales and the children? So, one of the first things you can ask yourself as you consider the State's manufactured time line is, why isn't Ms. Calderon there?

You can't make a time line in this case that makes any sense. No matter how you twist things, no matter how you contort things, unless you pick and choose what portions of a statement and what portions of testimony you're going to consider.

Now, you get to decide the credibility that you should give each witness. And in a case like this, that can be a very, very difficult thing to do. It's not as if we have clergymen coming in here and taking the stand. People that you might assume know the truth and that truth has some meaning to it.

And I'm reminded of something that I think all of us have heard when growing up. You should always tell the truth. Because if you tell the truth, you never have to worry about what it is you said when someone asks you again what it was that happened.

If you apply that standard to these, the testimony of many of these witnesses, did they tell the truth? And if they didn't tell truth, please, ask yourself, how is it you're supposed to decide when it is they're telling the truth? Will it be when it's convenient to the State's theory of the case, and everything that is said that fits in a time line? Well, that must be the truth. And everything else, well, you can just ignore because it does not make sense.

I submit to you, that's not how you view witnesses' testimony. You have to take it in the totality of the testimony. And one of [sic] things you can ask yourself is, if you take away the testimony of, if you take away the testimony of Reina Gonzales, what is the State's proof here?

If you just disregard what Reina Gonzales said — and I sat last night going through my notes of her various statements. And I'm sure you watched as I flipped through paperwork when she was on the stand, trying to find all the different things she said. And I flipped through my notes of her testimony.

And I thought it was going to be important for me to come in here before you with a list of all the lies that she told, and all the inconsistencies and statements that she made. And I realized I couldn't do it. I couldn't do it. And if I tried to do it, I'd still be talking next Wednesday.

And with the time we've spent here, I know the last thing you want me to do is still be talking next Wednesday going through the lies of Reina Gonzales. So I said, you know, these jurors have been paying attention. They have to have heard the lies.

They have to understand that this woman, this woman was charged with the same counts that Chris is charged with. Capital, first degree murder. She was facing a death sentence. She—we asked her about it. And I may or may not be able to find it if we dig through all these pieces of paper that we used over the weeks. She was facing two possible death sentences, a 70-year minimum sentence, on the two counts of first degree murder. It was life, death, or natural life, or life with parole after 35 years; with separate victims, it would be 70 years.

She testified that she was facing, she thought she was facing the same thing on the child abuse. So she was looking at a choice, by taking 22 years, of getting out when she's 45, potentially still young enough to have a child of her own, or potentially to meet up with a man who still has children, or going to trial and not getting out until she's 92. And she decided she'd give a new statement. And she assures you that this is now the truth. How do we know that?

The Judge says you can consider the witness' bias. You can consider the witness' motive in testifying. You've got yourself, looks like 70, well, 48 years worth of motive. And do you think that it is a coincidence that the story that she then tells shows up here for the State's time line? But even then you have to pick and choose which truth she tells you to try and make it fit.

You have to take the scissors to her testimony. And listen to State's counsel tell you, well, this is the part that's important, and this is the part that's true. So I'll put it on my time line. The other parts I won't. You can't do that.

You have Debra Reyes. Debra Reyes, the heroin dealer. Debra Reyes the 15 to, what is it, 10 to 15 grams of heroin a day, intravenously injected, working with her associates that she doesn't want to name because she's in the trade, the business of selling heroin. She's got prior felonies convictions. I made note of them somewhere. I won' t dig it out. But it was more than one.

That's the other piece of the State's puzzle here. But until you snip it, and listen to Ms. Eazer tell you what's important and what's not, her story doesn't fit with Reina Gonzales' story. Even the detective acknowledged that heroin addicts aren't the most reliable of sources. But, you're to base your opinion, you're to base the facts that you find on the heroin addicts in this case, because the State tell [sic] us that's the explanation that makes sense, because it fits if you solve the puzzle that way.

Terry White. Terry White didn't make the time line. Terry White testified that she went over at Easter to deliver cascarones to the children. And, you know, clearly she cares for Christopher. Clearly, you know, she stopped to say that. She came up to the stand. She talked about going over there. And she then was asked if she went over again. And she said, oh, yeah, I did. When was that, Ms. Eazer asked? Well, it was in August. How do you know it was in August? Because I took him tamales.

Now, in Tucson we know that August is when we get the green corner [sic] tamales, so that's something that makes sense. And that that wasn't what the State was looking for at that point in time, because they wanted to talk about the trip over there in June when she knocked on the door and nobody answered the door, because that fits in with the time line. But August doesn't. But what's significant about that in August?

She doesn't smell anything at the front door. She doesn't smell anything at the apartment. There's no testimony that — I think she was asked about that. She said, no, I didn't smell anything. Well, that doesn't fit in with the theory of the State's case. Now, I don't doubt that the inside of the house stank. You heard testimony that there were 20 bags, 20 Hefty bags worth of garbage in that place. There's no doubt that Reina Gonzales was not the best of housekeepers.

Seems that one of the things that is true about Reina's statement is that she spent the whole time getting high. So, if Chris is out sealing [sic] heroin, again, it's not a job we aspire towards, it's not a job that is considered appropriate employment. But it is what he was doing to, in his own way, try to provide and keep a roof over people's heads. But there's no dispute that he was gone all day, every day, from very early in the morning until very late at night.

So, if Reina Gonzales is at the apartment by herself, and Terry White comes over and knocks on the door, and Reina Gonzales is smoking heroin, do you expect Reina Gonzales to get up and answer the door for Chris' aunt?

If Forrest Payne comes over and knocks on the door, do you expect Reina Gonzales to get up, answer the door for him? You can decide that for yourself. But does the fact that the door isn't answered prove that at that point in time Chris is inside telling

Reina to keep people quiet? Only if you believe Reina. And Reina has 48 years worth of reasons to tell you what she told you. Plain and simple. Plain and simple.

Everything I said was a lie until what I'm telling you now. And you should believe her because? Because she has no motive. Because she has no interest? Because she isn't saving her own trial? Because, you know, it's fine to stand in front of you and express outrage for these children. And we all should be outraged because children deserve better. There's no doubt about that. But ask yourselves, where was the Government's outrage when the plea agreement with Reina Gonzales was signed? Where was the Government's plea imploring you for accountability when the Government acted as Judge, and jury, and decided that this case was a case of second degree murder? It was absent. But it's trotted out for you today.

And you'll have a copy of this plea agreement. You can look through it. You can give it the weight that you think it deserves in assessing how much of the testimony of Reina Gonzales you want to believe. It seems that where it is convenient for the children to be in the closet, the children are in the closet. And where it's inconvenient for children to be in the closet, you don't hear about it. What can that tell you?

What can it tell you when the only information that you hear about that comes from Reina Gonzales? You heard Chris Payne's statement. There's some ugly parts to the statement. There's some parts that are clearly not truthful. There's some parts that are sad to watch. There's some parts that you just shake your head and wonder how a human being could reach this kind of a point.

It's called heroin. He was a heroin addict, too. And so I'm not suggesting to you that you view the statements that he makes differently than you view the other addicts in this case. If you wanted to disregard it entirely, that would be within your province.

But one of the things the Judge is going to ask or tell you is that you have to do is to consider the voluntariness of that statement, to consider the condition he was in, the things that he was told, what, if any, promises were made to him as he's making his statement, and deciding how much of his statement you want to rely on.

And again, the Government can pick out parts of it because they'll fit the theory. They'll fit the time line. You can put them into the puzzle that they're telling you they're solving. But there was a lot more in the statement than you heard.

You heard genuine shock when he was told that Tyler's body wasn't with Ariana's. You can take a look at that reaction and see where else in the statement he had similar reactions to things that the police officers told him. You can make your own assessments about things, and decide what happened.

Now, something else that the Judge has told you before, and he'll tell you again. And it's told to you because it's really the starting point for a jury in its deliberations. Mr. Payne is presumed by law to be innocent. He starts with—not starting even, he's starting presumed by law to be innocent. And that has to change through the evidence that's produced.

And again, I don't want to minimize, and I will not minimize what happened to the children. But you may ask yourselves, if Mr. Payne was leaving at seven or eight in the morning, we heard one person said seven, another, I think Reina, said by eight, Debra Reyes said by seven. And I think I perhaps told you, you can't believe a lot of what they say, maybe the stuff you can believe is stuff that relates to selling heroin. I really don't know.

But there's testimony that is pretty much undisputed that he was out of that apartment for the entire day, until late at night, for two months, I think the testimony was, that he was selling heroin full-time with Debra Reyes.

Now, again, we have some things that don't fit into the little puzzle. But Debra Reyes told you that she got Chris because he used to work with another associate. So the statement that Reina gave you that, well, after SKOR he was not working at all for a month or two, then he started to work with Debra Reyes, Debra Reyes says something to the contrary there. Because she tells us he was working with another associate.

The other thing that I didn't hear discussed because, again, you can't make sense of everything here and still stay with this time line, the phone calls. There's no dispute that Reina Gonzales was calling Chris Payne when Chris Payne worked at SKOR.

Again, one of the witnesses that you may be able to — that you can't discount as a heroin addict and someone whose credibility you can assess is George Sklias. And George came in, and George talked about the changes in Chris towards the end of his employment at SKOR. George talked about the phone calls. George talked about Chris going home. George talked about his knowledge of all of that. Now, that would seem to lead to a conclusion that, prior to April, Reina is calling because she's having trouble with the kids.

The other phone calls that you didn't hear about, Debra Reyes, talked about the phone calls coming in. That's because that presents a little bit of a problem to the time line. Because you see the time line has the children in the closet 24-7, not my words, someone else's, until they're dead. Starting, we're going to say, according to the time line in July, because one of our firm dates is knowing that Debra Reyes was bonded out of jail on that date.

Well, what did Debra Reyes say alternatively? I think I lived there in January. It might have been in March. No, I guess it was after I got bonded out of jail. I started living there, hum, couple of weeks, a month, not sure when, after I got bonded out of jail. And I stayed there either three weeks or two months, I really don't remember.

So from that, we now can conclude the children are in the closet 24-7. Even though some of the testimony that I recall is that, I think this was from Reina, that Chris was working full-time for Debra Reyes, after she was bonded out of the jail. Which would mean that for that two-month period of time, and now we're out to two months from June 22nd, if it's two months we' re out to August 22nd, during that period of time Reina is calling dozens of times a day. Problems with the children. Can hear the children crying and screaming in the background. These are from the children that are in the closet 24-7 until their deaths. That doesn't fit the State's theory, so we don' t put that on the time line.

But why would you disregard that part of Debra Reyes' testimony? Because if you disregard that, then it can fit into the puzzle that the State wants you to solve. And I'm not saying to you that you may be able to solve this puzzle. Certainly if this puzzle is supposed to be the State of Arizona has proven that Christopher Payne committed first degree murder, I will tell you that you will not solve the puzzle with the evidence that you received.

There's no evidence that Christopher Payne premeditated the death of these children. There's no evidence that Christopher Payne acted in a way that his actions were in the course of and in furtherance of child abuse, such that he intentionally or knowingly left his kid, placed his kid, did things to his children, in a way that would have exposed them to death or risk of serious physical injury.

He wasn't there. The Government might tell you that this is all about the choices that were made. Well, who made choices? Who made a choice to feed Chris Junior, if the children were in the closet when Chris is out selling heroin full-time with Debbie Reyes? When Reina Gonzales made breakfast, did she make breakfast for one child, or for three? When it was lunch time, did she make lunch for one child, or for three? When it was dinner time, does she make dinner for one child, or for three? That was the first day the children were in the closet, if they were when Reina says they were.

The second day. Chris gets up in the morning. He either picks up Debbie Reyes or she picks him up. They leave at 7:00 to begin the process of doing their deliveries, because heroin addicts have to have heroin. Have to have heroin every day. There's no doubt about that. You heard what happens when a heroin addict doesn't have heroin. You heard what withdrawal is. You heard the symptoms of that. You saw the symptoms of that when you looked at the video, okay.

What you saw was consistent with what the other witnesses said about how one is when one withdraws from heroin. So you know that calls are coming in through the deliveries. And they're out there, and that's the second day, when Reina Gonzales made breakfast for little Chris, she made a choice to make breakfast, for one, and not for three. When she made lunch, for one, and not for three. When she made dinner, for one, and not for three.

And the Government stands in front of you and says that Christopher Payne is more culpable than Reina Gonzales? The Government said that what Reina Gonzales did was second degree murder. And they tell you what Christopher Payne did by not being there is first degree murder? That doesn't make sense. In all of the important ways in which you make decisions, that does not make sense. And you know that that isn't right. It doesn't fit the time line, but first degree murder doesn't fit this.

Now, as Ms. McLean indicated in her opening statement, the defense is not asking you to absolve Christopher Payne from responsibility. The defense is not telling you that Christopher Payne was a good father, that the children were better off being with Christopher Payne.

But one of the questions that you have to ask yourself is, Child Protective Services saw what they saw with the condition of the children with Jamie Hallam. And Child Protective Services said to Christopher Payne, you should get custody of these children. And there's no dispute that he filled out custody paperwork because he showed it to the police department.

So, the notion that everything was fine and hunky-dory, I don't think is consistent with the common sense that Ms. Eazer

was thankful that you all had, that you bring into these deliberations in deciding this case. It just—it isn't consistent with that.

Now, the other thing that, while I'm on this, the Government
can't tell you when the children died, because no one knows. And
because they can't tell you when the children died, you can't even
begin to guess at when Ariana's bones were broken, or how they
were broken.

One of [sic] things that Reina Gonzales says is that she never
saw Chris do anything that would be consistent with the breaking of bones. The Government would have you side step that by
saying, well, Chris would take them into the bedroom to punish
them, and Reina wouldn't see what was going on. But, wouldn't
this be when the children were in the closet 24-7? So he's going to
take them out of the closet to punish them while Reina goes to the
other room? There's no evidence of that.

And, quite frankly, if Reina Gonzales is, in essence, thrown
[sic] Chris Payne under the bus to save her own skin, and I think
there's real good evidence that that's what's going on here, you
think she might have said, oh, yeah, and by the way I saw him
break these ribs, and I heard the child cry, et cetera, et cetera, et
cetera. Because at that point what does she have to lose by saying
that?

So, perhaps the fact that she didn't say that, is reasonable evidence that that didn't happen then. And the Government says,
well, you don't have to worry about that because Dr. Anderson
said up to eight weeks—up to eight months. And the eight months
would be, would be a stretch.

Well, you heard his testimony. You can decide what it is he said
about the time line. But you also heard him say that he would defer
to somebody who had greater expertise. And I asked him, oh, do
you mean somebody who might be a pediatrician, or a pathologist,
a pediatric pathologist? And he said, absolutely.

And you had heard from a pediatric pathologist, Dr. Ophoven.
And the Government would have you believe that, I think the ex-

act words were, she's here to try and stretch things. I'm not sure exactly, something to that effect. And there's just absolutely no evidence of that.

Because she told you that in her opinion, in her knowledge, based upon science, you don't determine the age of a fracture by the amount of callus in a bone. You're looking at a process of re-forming of the bone. That when it is complete, allows you to probably not be able to see that the original fracture happened. And that that process of remodeling includes looking to see if the marrow had regenerated where the break was, and other things like that.

And she told you that she really, she—neither she nor anybody can date fractures by looking at fractures. But that the fractures would be healed—this is up here somewhere, too—return to previous state a year plus.

So, first off, if, if the children died sometime in August, then up to a year brings us back to the preceding summer. And we only heard reports about how the children were with CPS and with family members from October on.

And we aren't here to guess and speculate, the Judge will tell you, though it seems that even in considering much of the arguments that have been made, that's exactly what you've been asked to do.

So, we can't tell when the bones were broken. And if you don't know, then you certainly can't convict a man of breaking those bones. And when is it he's supposed to have broken them? Up to and including August when Carolina Calderon is there watching the kids, telling us that the children appeared to be normal? Telling us that the children don't seem to have what she — she didn't describe anything that was wrong other than the bruise. And I'm, excuse me, there was clearly something wrong, the child was bruised, but she isn't describing broken bones. So how do we make sense of that?

How do we make sense of the Government telling you that, well, gee, Ariana probably died while Debbie Reyes was living in the apartment, whenever that was, because there was some sort of a commotion in the bedroom and, therefore, that was when Chris was freaking out. How can that be, if they're still working full-time during that period, and Reina is calling dozens of times a day? And you can hear the children screaming and crying in the background. And I think she said that she could hear three children. Not one, not two, but three.

So, where does that leave you? It certainly doesn't leave you with a neat, orderly time line. It certainly doesn't leave you with a firm conclusion that the State has proven first degree murder, either by premeditation, or by felony murder.

Because, suppose, suppose, suppose that Reina did not care for Jamie Hallam's children. Is there evidence of that? Absolutely. She said so herself. And one of the things that you can consider is that there were three children in that apartment. The one that survived it was the one with Reina Gonzales' DNA.

Does that mean that Chris made good choices? No. Does that mean that Chris Payne should have done something different? Absolutely. But suppose that this man, misguided in his work though he was, had that old-fashioned notion that he's leaving to go work in the morning, and that the woman who is the mother of his third child would take care of his other children as well while he was gone. And suppose that Reina's way of taking care of the three children was to begin to put them in the closet.

She'll tell you that Chris did that, or told her to do that, but she can't tell you when. She can't tell you why. But suppose that the children spend increasing time in the closet. And Mr. Payne makes assumptions about how they're being treated that aren't right. And that when he comes home at 11:00, the children are asleep. Or his children have been terrorized by Reina during the day because, you know, we only have Reina's word on this, that Chris is the one who did the terrible things that she says he did.

But suppose Reina Gonzales is the one who systematically deprived the children of nourishment, as they become weaker, and weaker, and wither away. And their father, the heroin addict, lacks the wherewith all [sic] to have an understanding of what's going on.

He, like Reina, like Debra Reyes, isn't thinking of anything beyond getting high, smoking his heroin a couple of times a day. However many times it was. And he has an extreme indifference to the health of those children. Does that mean he's committing first degree murder and premeditating their deaths? Having a plan. Says, yes, I think I'll lock these children in the closet until they starve to death. Do you believe that's what this evidence shows?

Because if you do, you have to cut the pieces of the witnesses' testimony to make them fit, and to ignore other testimony that you hear about this case.

We also had the neighbor, I apologize for not remembering his name for you, it's in my notes. But he didn't hear people coming and going. He never saw people living there at the apartment. And his bedroom window was by the top of the stairs. He smelled a smell. It was garbage. He complained about it. No doubt there was garbage there. There was plenty of evidence of that.

But, just suppose that Christopher Payne Senior really didn't know what a cold-hearted, evil woman Reina Gonzales was. Suppose that Christopher Payne Senior didn't know the extent to which Reina Gonzales did not want his children to be there. Did not welcome the children there. Resented the fact that someone else's children were there when it should just be her child and her boyfriend, Christopher. And suppose she then began treating these children differently.

Now, does that mean that Chris is intentionally or knowingly committing child abuse, and that these deaths are in the course of and in further — and in furtherance of, not just in the course of, and in furtherance of the child abuse? Or does that mean that he was reckless in his conduct? And that, of course, presupposes that you have found that he knew what Reina Gonzales was doing while he wasn't there.

And the Government has said that what Reina Gonzales did was second degree murder. You heard testimony that because of starvation, if starvation is how they died, that the children could have been saved literally up until the last minute if someone had intervened. And, you know, we all know, because of our common sense, we all know heroin addicts are not good parents, and that's why we have CPS. And the tragedy is that no one saw these children to intervene in time.

But Reina Gonzales was there, day after day after day after day after day. That was her conduct. And the Government asks to you find Chris Payne more culpable.

I submit to you that Chris Payne is culpable in this case. Chris Payne committed second degree murder. He was negligent. He was reckless. He had an extreme indifference to the health of the children, to the safety of the children, to whether the condition the children were in were [sic] such that they would live or they would die. And he was reckless in not appreciating that he needed to do something different as the children got thinner and thinner.

But you also heard testimony that if a person is deprived of fluid, the end comes really quickly, couple of days. So if the children have been weakened by Reina Gonzales systematically depriving them of food, and you'll notice she did slip in her story because she told you Chris was feeding them, well, how does that fit? But, suppose she then stops giving them any liquid. And we don't have, as Ms. Eazer indicated to you, this long prolonged suffering. It's something that is quicker. Again, did these children deserve this? Absolutely not. But does the fact of the children's death, and horrifying way in which it may have occurred, mean that the Government has proven intentional first degree murder, or felony murder in this case, based upon intentional or knowing child abuse? Not under these circumstances. Not under these circumstances, members of the jury.

Because, you have to pick. You have to choose. You have to snip it away. And you have to make it fit. And the time line is inconsistent with itself. You heard me ask the officer if he took Reina Gonzales' statement, and looked at a calendar, and there was [sic] calendar there for you. And then you took Debra Reyes' statement and you looked at a calendar, and you started marking dates down on the calendar. Would you wind up with the same events on the same dates? And he said, no.

Well, I submit to you, that if you took their statements and you took the calendar, and you started at one end and worked forward, and you started at the other end and worked backwards, with each individual person you'd have a completely different time line. And the Government's solution to that is to tell you, you don't need to reconcile that, just pick and choose.

Now, the other thing that I have to talk to you about [sic] little bit, because it really doesn't fit what I submit to you is the real puzzle that you just can't solve here, and solve it where it says first degree murder, is that there are other things that the Government did that really have nothing to do with any of this case. And the prime example of that would be searching the dump.

Not that it matters for what you're here to decide, but the fact of the matter is if the police officers who responded to the scene of the original finding of the body there at the U-Store-It, if those officers had properly processed the crime scene, which includes climbing into the dumpster to see if anything else might be in the dumpster, then there wouldn't have been need to go out to the dump and search the dump, because they would have found the evidence that was there.

And maybe you'd have had different evidence, maybe not. We don't know. They might say, well, there wasn't any reason to expect there was anything else in the dumpster. That's a really unfortunate explanation for why we did not bother to climb up and check.

But, the dumpster testimony, I thought, was interesting, in the way that it may apply to what you're almost being asked to do with some of the State's case here. The detective said that when they would search the dump, because there had been additional loads that had been brought, they had to use a big bucket to pick it up and put it into a dump truck, drive it to either place and spread it, dump it, spread it all out, mark a grid, and then walk the skirmish line to see what they could find.

They talked about using cadaver dogs to see if they could find any human remains, and that didn't work. Because, gosh, you know, there's so many dirty diapers and other things that cadaver dogs would respond to, that it was a waste of time. And after the second trip out there, they decided they weren't going to allocate anymore [sic] resources to what they thought would be a waste of time.

Well, the State's case really is not that different than picking up that load of garbage from the dump and bringing it into the courtroom and spreading it out and saying, well, now let's walk through this. And we'll ignore the lies, because there's some truth here that we can find. I'll show you where it is. That's not the way you decide a criminal case.

You have to consider all of the evidence. You have to consider all of the witnesses. You have to consider their motives. You have to consider their bias. You have to consider what they bring into this courtroom.

And one of the most, to me, interesting answers that was heard, was when Reina Gonzales was on the stand, towards the end, in hindsight, I wish I had been counting the lies so I could tell you how many there had been. But it was towards the end, and Ms. Eazer said to her, well, why didn't you do something. And her answer was, I don't know.

And please, because this case all depends on that woman's testimony. Remember how she was up there? Is that what you said? I don't remember. Well, if you saw a transcript of a recording of what you said, would that refresh your memory? Maybe. No. Do you remember saying this? Maybe. No. Yes. I mean, she was all over the place with that. She was hostile. She was angry.

Did she, did her testimony resonate with you? With the clarity of truth? Was it the story that you know it's true because you just hear it and it has that ring, like a bell? It's clear, it's bright. It's the same every time you say it? No.

Now, the Government's answer to this is, well, you know, even though she might have had all of the statements that were made, she said some things that weren't in the statement. She told us all about the closet. Why would she have done that? Well, could it be because she knew she needed to tell a good story?

Could it be because she knew from the evidence that she'd heard about, that they had done DNA testing and they found swabs and taken swabs and proved that certain DNA profiles were located in the closet? So, boy, oh, boy, if I tell them about a closet, gosh, you know, I know my DNA is in there, too. But heck, I was living in the apartment. But I can just say that the kids were in the closet, and that will make everything work out.

So, what if that didn't happen? What if that is a creation from an evil woman who bore malice to those two children and acted on that malice? And to save herself, told this story about Chris.

This story that doesn't fit the stories of others, because, gosh, you know, Chris Payne was either working full-time for Debra Reyes either before or after that 6-22 bail out date. Debra Reyes either lived there or didn't, depending on whether you believed the neighbor. And we don't know when that was. We don't know for how long that was. What is that?

I submit to you that what you're fairly left with, is the conclusion that, in this case of tragedy, in this case of loss, undeserved loss, in this case in which innocent children, and there's, I can't find them readily, there's photographs of the children that were admitted into evidence. You'll see them, and it's truly heartbreaking. This is a heartbreaking case. This a case that will stay with you for the rest of your lives. But in this case do you find Chris Payne is more culpable than Reina Gonzales?

When the Judge and jurors in her case said that, everything that you did, every time that you fed Chris Junior and you didn't feed Ariana and Tyler, every day that went by, according to your story, if that's what happened at all, every day that went by, that you didn't care for those children, that you made a choice not to do that, that was second degree murder.

Remember the phone calls? Debra Reyes, our heroin dealer, she would get angry because Chris would, he was the driver, she had no control. He would run home to try and deal with the situation. Is that because Reina Gonzales was dealing with the situation? I think didn't Debra Reyes even say [sic], you know, you need to take care of your own business here.

What if Reina Gonzales took care of her business? Took care of her business in a way that Chris was reckless about, was extremely indifferent to, but that he did not know what she was doing to Chris and what was happening in his own apartment. It's easy enough to say he lived there, he should have known. But there's a difference between saying he lived there, he should have known, and saying the Government has presented me with proof that this is what is so.

You're not here to speculate. You're not here to guess. You're not here to be told that, well, because we don't have direct evidence, there must be circumstantial evidence, and your speculations are the same as circumstantial evidence and, therefore, if you can cut the pieces of the puzzle up, so that they fit into my time line, then it's first degree murder and that's what, you know, you're implored to do.

You're asked to bring your common sense, to bring your good judgment, to bring your collective wisdom, to bring your assessment of the witnesses, their motives, their statements, the consistencies and inconsistencies, as it fits with the entire picture.

With the entire picture. Because there's little things that happened throughout the case that, you know, sometimes I'm sure you got frustrated with me because it seems like I was always interrupting things, asking to come up and talk to the Judge about things. And I trust you'll understand that there are reasons why lawyers have to do the things that they do in a courtroom at times.

But we had this discussion with several different witnesses about luminol, about DNA, and about, I think it was positive for blood, or preliminary showing for blood. And the police officer wanted to tell you because of the luminol that there was blood here and there was blood there. And then that changed, and it was suspected blood. And then the gentleman who came in and did the luminol test told you that it's a presumptive test for blood and needs to be confirmed at the laboratory.

And then you heard that the laboratory did a preliminary test for blood, and confirmed a preliminary test for blood. Then you heard that there were confirmatory tests for blood, and that at least in the opinion of one of the experts who came in, Ms. Feriesan, who testified about DNA and laboratory and tests that you do, until you do the confirmatory tests for blood, you cannot say that it was blood because there are other things that will give you these sorts of positive readings.

And you heard that there were cleansers, there were just a whole list of things that could give you positive readings when you're looking at luminol.

Now, the Government would like you to just take that leap with them, that because the police officer says blood when it's really suspected blood, and because there's a glow in a closet that was, I think there's testimony was sprayed with carpet cleaner, and, therefore, there must be blood in the closet. And, gosh, you know, that's consistent with Reina Gonzales saying that there was a head wound on Tyler Payne, because there was a head wound and that's why the blood got in the closet and it all fits and your job here is done.

Well, you also heard testimony that head wounds bleed profusely. And again, that's something you know from your common sense. And if the children were in the closet 24-7, there wasn't any testimony that, well, let's keep Tyler out of the closet while his head is bleeding so that he doesn't make a mess on the rug in the carpet in the closet.

So, you can take a look at the photographs and you can see if there's copious amounts of blood, or even visible amounts of blood that would allow you to conclude that that part of that statement is true. It's yet another inconsistency that doesn't make it on to the State's time line.

And the thing that I really cannot underscore enough, members of this jury, is that you should ask yourself why it is that at the times that matter, the people who make the time line are the junkies, and the sober people, Carolina Calderon, didn't tell you that she was doing drugs, Terry White wasn't doing drugs, George Sklias wasn't doing drugs, the neighbor wasn't doing drugs, nothing that they have to say makes the time line.

This case, such that it is, is based upon the testimony of liars, and junkies. And liars and junkies do not warrant a conviction. Their testimony does not warrant a conviction for first degree murder. It cannot be relied relayed [sic] on. You're permitted to discount it. And if you can't reconcile it, then this case has not been proven. And I submit to you that under any reasonable analysis of those witnesses' statements, you cannot reconcile that testimony.

What you do know, is that the kids deserve better. And you do know that Chris Payne Senior did not give them the care, the attention, the awareness to their situation that he owed them. He failed. He failed.

But do you believe for a moment that he called CPS, which he did, because CPS told him to change custody. And he filled out paperwork, and you heard evidence about that. He showed the paperwork to the police. So, Jamie Hallam knows where the police are—or excuse me, knows where the children are. CPS knows where the children are. The police know where the children are. The people that he works with at SKOR know where the children are.

Do you think that Christopher Payne then thought, well, you know, I think it would be a good idea just to lock these children in the closet and let them starve to death?

Now, I know junkies don't always have good ideas, but even that stretches the realm of credibility. That is so far beyond the pale that I submit to you that you can reject this.

And the other thing that should get noted, and again, Chris Payne has a responsibility here that you will decide. But many, many people during those months could and should have done something. Ms. Hallam went over there in March to get her kids back, and that didn't work, because of CPS.

A CPS woman who went through a lot while she was on the stand, but was careful to say the children appeared fine physically, CPS made a mistake. CPS—I'll get back to that.

But CPS said, leave the children with Jamie, or with Christopher. And it's really, for purposes of what we do here today, it really doesn't matter whether or not the officer's statement that CPS told me to do that, or the CPS woman's statement that, well, there you have your answer, referring to the paperwork, is true, because it doesn't, it doesn't matter. But that was in March.

Did you hear any evidence that Ms. Hallam ever went back to the police? Or back to CPS? Or back to the apartment at any day thereafter? No. Now, that does not make the deaths her fault, and I'm not trying to say that. But that is an example of this perfect storm of inattention and failure that contributed to the deaths of these innocent children.

So, CPS got to buy their way out by paying a million dollars, so that they didn't have a trial. Reina Gonzales, she got to lie her way out, so that she didn't have to have a trial.

And what I'm asking you to do with this case, members of the jury, is to apply the law as it fits to these facts, once you've determined the facts, and to find that Chris Payne, who is here on trial, is not any more culpable than Reina Gonzales in his actions.

Thank you very much.

What is important about the Mr. Obrien's statement is the fact that the jury can decide whether Chris's statement to the police was voluntary or not, and if they decide if it wasn't, then the statement can be thrown out.

Sue has the last rebuttal, and she mainly points out that the defense has mentioned a lot of what if's, should'ves, could'ves, and theories in their closing argument. She tells the jurors to stay with the evidence of the time-lines and to find Christopher Payne guilty on all counts of 1st degree murder and the underlying charges.

Judge Fields then tells the jury that it's now time to deliberate. He tells them to vote on a foreman once they're sequestered for the deliberations. He then reads them instructions of the law and afterwards tells them to follow the bailiff into their room. The court is dismissed, except for the attorneys, who are to meet with the judge in his chambers.

I go back to the office and wait. For me, this is a very nervous time. You never know how a jury will vote; when you think you have a sure case and think it's a slam dunk, sometimes you don't get the result you expected, for one reason or another. It's now a waiting game. Sue and her staff have my cell phone number and will call me immediately when the verdict is in. Mike tells me he wants to go to the courtroom with me when the verdict comes in.

Verdict & Penalty

··

Day 15: Tuesday, March 17, 2009

The jury is out most of the morning and part of the afternoon. At about 2:45 p.m. I receive several calls from the County Attorneys Office, Sue among them. She tells me the verdict is in. I tell Mike, and we immediately walk over to the courthouse. The courtroom is quickly filling up with media and staff and family members on both sides. Jamie is a few rows in back of me.

Once the courtroom is settled, Judge Fields comes in and addresses the courtroom. He tells everyone to keep his or her comments and emotions in check during and after the verdict. He then calls for the jury. The bailiff brings them in, and everyone stands as they file in and take their seats. The Judge addresses them and asks the foreperson if they have come to a decision. The foreman says they have, and hands the bailiff the letter. It's presented to the Judge first, and then to the court clerk. She stands up and begins to read it.

Everything seems surreal to me, and chills are rolling through my spine and neck. I look at Chris. He has never made any emotional gesture towards anything up to now. I look toward the court clerk as she reads the verdict.

She states, "We, the jury, find the defendant, Christopher Payne, guilty on count one, 1st degree murder of Ariana Payne." She says, "We, the jury, find the defendant guilty on count two, child abuse on Ariana Payne." She says, "We, the jury, find the defendant, Christopher Payne, guilty on count three, child abuse on Ariana Payne." She says, "We, the jury, find the defendant, Christopher Payne, guilty on count four, hiding or concealing a dead body on Ariana Payne." She says, "We, the jury, find the defendant, Christopher Payne, guilty on count five, 1st degree murder of Tyler Payne." She says, "We, the jury, find the defendant guilty on count six, child abuse on Tyler Payne." She says, "We, the jury, find the defendant, Christopher Payne, guilty on count seven, child abuse on Tyler Payne." She says, "We, the jury, find the defendant, Christopher Payne, guilty of count eight, hiding or concealing a dead body on Tyler Payne."

I am overwhelmed, but stay in check. Judge Fields asks Mr. O'Brien if he wants to poll the jurors. He does, and they unanimously agree with their decision of guilt on all of the counts. Judge Fields then tells the jury that they need to deliberate on the death penalty eligibility on Chris Payne. The jury is given about a half-hour break while he speaks to the attorneys on both sides on the next step that needs to be taken.

When everyone returns, the jury is sent back to deliberate for the mitigating and aggravating phase. The jurors return with a verdict in thirty minutes. The clerk reads the letter, and they have decided he is eligible for the death penalty. Once this has come in and is read, Judge Fields decides to excuse the jurors for the rest of the day and move into the mitigating and aggravating segment of the trial in the morning.

Day 16: Wednesday, March 18, 2009

This is the Penalty Phase.

The court reconvenes, and the jury is brought back. In this phase of the trial, the defense has the burden of proof and will lead off with the opening statements.

Rebecca McLean opens by stating that Chris was loved by his family, but had a "disrupted" childhood, and his problems started in the early years of his childhood. She says his mother, Socorro, passed away when he was four months old, after which his father began drinking and was depressed.

Chris was neglected and passed from family member to family member. At one point, there were family issues when an aunt blamed him for the death of his mother. Eventually, this was resolved, and everyone moved on. This had a negative impact on his life.

He was, however, a good student in his early years. As he moved into his high school years, he got into drugs, but did have a job at a nursing home. The family put Chris in a rehabilitation center. He struggled back and forth with the drugs.

His father remarried, and now he had two stepsisters and a stepmother. When Chris was older, he married Jamie, and they had Tyler and Ariana. They eventually divorced, and later he met Reina Gonzales. Together, they had a baby. Chris knew that Jamie had a drug problem and knew that CPS was trying to take the kids. He then took them because he thought that he was the better parent.

Chris got a job (with SKOR) and did well at first, but his addiction to heroin caught up to him, and he lost his job. She says that an expert will testify on how his upbringing contributed to his downfall. She says that this is a sad tale and hopes that, considering all the circumstances, the jury will consider the life sentence.

It's now Sue's opportunity to address the jurors in her closing statements. She declines and asks to defer her closing statement to a later time. She says that, at this time, Jamie wants to address the court and read a letter she's written. Jamie reads the following to the court:

Dear Honorable Judge Fields,

There are no words to describe the pain, anger, and despair that I've felt from Tyler and Ariana's murders. I have not only lost one child, but also I have lost two. My babies were the most amazing and wonderful children any mother could ever have. They loved each other so much and had a bond that was inseparable and their personalities were so sweet and gentle.

Please allow me a few minutes to tell you about Ariana and Tyler. They were like night and day, though. Ariana would go to bed early; Tyler liked to stay up late. He would wake Ariana up if she was sleeping and he was awake. She loved milk with her food; he drank juice. He liked to be everywhere I was. Ariana was more independent. She would play by herself and be comfortable with it, but she was very cuddly. She would sit on my lap for hours and didn't move. I can still hear her little voice in my head saying, "I LOOVVE YOUU." It was such a sweet gentle voice.

Tyler was particular in what he ate and he loved to cook! He would often play outside in the back yard with his trucks and cars. Tyler loved to cook and loved Scooby-Doo. He had Scooby-Doo bed sheets and t-shirts and every video possible that had Scooby-Doo. He liked to ride his bike (with training wheels, of course). Tyler was a true mamma's boy.

Ariana's favorite activity most of all was coloring. She had a little bag that she would carry everywhere. Before we went anywhere she would make sure that it was stocked up with her paper and her crayons and coloring pencils.

She would put pens, markers, and even chalk in that little bag—anything that she could color with. She just loved all the different colors. She would fall asleep coloring on most nights. She also loved to eat. Often times, she would eat everything on her plate, then move into Tyler's seat and eat the rest of his meal.

It saddens me to know that my precious little boy and my sweet little girl were treated so cruel. Ariana and Tyler's murders took everything from me. It took my security and my innocence; it took my rest and my peace. I have lost my faith and trust in people.

I have trouble finding joy in the simple pleasures of life. Being "happy" doesn't seem right anymore. Sometimes the feeling of despair becomes so overwhelming, so oppressive, that it literally takes my breath away.

I never know what sound or what sight is going to trigger a memory in my mind. And when the memories of Ariana and Tyler are so sweet, with them comes the realization that they are gone and each time that realization hits my heart it is devastating.

I understand why Sue deferred her closing statement and instead had Jamie read her letter. I think this was a brilliant move on her part. At the end of Jamie's letter, the courtroom is quiet and emotional. It doesn't matter what was said in the closing statement by the defense. No one remembers. Instead, they're thinking of these wonderful children and how a mother never deserved to lose them.

Day 17: Thursday, March 19, 2009

The trial continues, and the defense calls in a parade of family and friends to testify on Chris Payne's behalf. All of them speak about his problems growing up and his drug addiction. Some of his co-workers also testify. All the testimony is consistent. Later on, the defense calls in their expert witness, Thomas Reidy. At the conclusion of the day's testimony, the jurors are sent home for the next four days, including the weekend. They are to report at 9:00 a.m. on Tuesday.

Days 18-23:
Tuesday, March 24 to Tuesday, March 31, 2009

Dr. Thomas Reidy is a mitigation expert who testifies in death penalty cases. He's a psychologist and evaluated Chris for a short time only. After getting information about Chris's background and speaking with him, he says that his upbringing had a negative impact on his life.

Sue then picks him apart in her rebuttal. What she stresses is the amount of time he spent on the reports that he was given by the defense. With limited information and limited time spent with Chris, how could he possibly conduct a proper evaluation?

More of Chris Payne's family and friends testify throughout the rest of the week.

Day 23: Tuesday, March 31, 2009

Both attorneys present their facts as to why Chris should or shouldn't get the death penalty. The judge again reads the jurors the instructions and sends them to deliberate. I hang out around the courthouse, speak with Sue and her staff, and then go back to the office.

After three hours, I receive a call from Sue, telling me the jury is back. I return to the courtroom. Judge Fields again tells the court to keep composed; he doesn't want a reaction to the verdict. The bailiff brings in the jurors. The letter is given to Judge Fields, and then to the clerk.

She states, "We, the jury, do sentence Christopher Payne to death in the murder of Ariana Payne." She continues and says, "We, the jury, do sentence Christopher Payne to death in the murder of Tyler Payne." The jurors are again polled at the request of the defense, and again it is unanimous.

I feel the same chill going down my spine. I look at Chris. He is unemotional and doesn't even look up. I see Chris's parents, Forrest and Pat Payne, immediately leave the courtroom. Judge Field thanks the jurors for their service and excuses them. They're now allowed to talk about the case if they want to.

I can't express the feelings I have. I go outside the courtroom. I see Jamie huddled with her family and members of Sue's staff. I go over to Jamie. She looks at me, and I tell her I'm happy for her and with the verdict. She smiles halfway. I also apologize to her for not being able to find Tyler. She tears up and hugs me. The media is also in the hallway, and they take a picture of this moment. We all go into one of the vacant jury rooms. Jamie says she wants all of us to meet at the Children's Memorial Park. A time is set up to meet there.

As I'm leaving, I'm approached by some of the jurors. They tell me I did a good job, and that it was a horrific case to work. I thank them and tell them it means a lot to hear that from them. As we're walking out of the courthouse, the media is still around, trying to get interviews. They speak to Sue, and she gives them a statement.

They approach me for a statement. I'm asked if this is a case that will stay with me. I smile and say that it will. I'm then asked how I deal with the stress of investigating this type of case. I don't answer that. I'm then asked if Chris has any redeeming qualities. I tell them, "With Chris, he had every opportunity to do right for those kids, the way he did it was his choosing, this was what he did, and this was his punishment. No! He does not have any redeeming qualities." As I'm walking back to the office, I call my wife and relay the news. She's relieved and happy it's over.

I meet everyone at the Children's Memorial Park. Jamie has balloons she wants us to release to the children. She points to the inscribed names of Tyler and Ariana on the wall. As we gather, she reads a letter to all of us:

Yesterday many children cried out in pain.
Yesterday many heard that cry but chose to ignore it.
Yesterday many children died from child abuse.
Yesterday many had to live in guilt for ignoring their pain.
Yesterday many children went to Heaven while many still suffer.
Yesterday many felt the heartache of losing a child.

Today one child's silent voice will be heard.
Today one more person will stand up for them.
Today one child won't cry out in pain.
Today one person heard that child's cry but chose to do something.
Today one child was saved from death.
Today one person felt proud because they saved a life.
Today one child will make it.
Today one person will do their part.

What is the difference between yesterday and today?
One person making a change.
One person standing up for a child.
One compared to many
May not be big to you and me,
But to a child, one person made the difference
Between Life & Death for them.
If you believe in it, stand for it.
The most promising truth of all:
Yesterday many spoke of change
Today one will do something about it.
Many will speak of change
But there are very few who will do something about it.
Never doubt that a small group of committed people can change
    the world.
Indeed, it's the only thing that everyone has.
The world is a dangerous place
Not because of those who do the evil
But because of those who look on, and do nothing about it.[1]

---

[1] This poem was sent to Jamie, but the author is unknown.

THE AFTERMATH

TYLER, JAMIE, AND ARIANA

I am telling this story to bring awareness to child abuse and how terrible it is. There are options to counter this, and we as a community need to report it and protect the children. I found out that then Senator Jonathan Paton attended the trial and afterwards was instrumental in making changes to the laws that govern Child Protective Services. State Bill HB 2455 was passed. This created tighter regulations that have been put in place, holding CPS more accountable to these children and requiring them to work with law enforcement to ensure that this type of tragedy will not happen again.

I know that Tyler and Ariana, through their deaths, did have a positive effect. I believe they did either save Jamie's life or, at the very least, help her to conquer her demons. Jamie is now a positive influence and a spokesperson advocate for the prevention of child abuse. Jamie is an amazing person because of the way she turned her life around.

This is the true story of the death of innocents.

CPSIA information can be obtained at www.ICGtesting.com
Printed in the USA
BVOW082356180213

313593BV00002B/3/P